redtail reprint series

golden gate

interviews with 5 san francisco poets

edited by
david meltzer

wingbow press

Contents

golden gate

Re-Surface

Originally I planned a book four times as big as the one you're holding, a book of interviews representing three generations of San Francisco poetry, concluding with a round-table discussion on what's right and wrong with what is called San Francisco poetry and this discussion would have been (rightfully) between younger poets who have had to learn their art in an over-historicized millieu.

In a way I am glad my largesse diminished in response to the book which did emerge because there can never be a comprehensive and totally democratic book on anything, especially poetry.

I'm also happy to say that poetry is flourishing in the Bay Area as never before. Not only diverse groups of survivors and elders who, like myself, are considered representative by repetition of name, but levels and degrees of poets learning and practising their craft in perfect accord with their capacities. Never has the region been more open and responsive to its poetries. There seems to exist for almost every poet an audience, even if it's one other person. Poets with specific or transitional voices can find teachers and disciples easily enough. There are workshops and coffee houses and platforms for poets to share ideas, read each others work. Publishing has exploded due to the new print technologies; almost anyone can and will publish their work and there will be someone out there to read it. Poets are on the radio. They are in public schools teaching poetry to children, they are in state and city colleges teaching and reading and conducting workshops. They are functioning in shamanic and ceremonial capacities. Poets are restoring the strength of ethnic traditions and, as always, opening the doors to the future of self and tribe. The Bay Area is continuously enriched by its poetry which is a fact any poet who comes here becomes immediately aware of.

I would like to dedicate this re-issue of SAN FRAN-CISCO POETS to the memory of Lew Welch whose works I'd hoped the original printing would serve. I had thought that when the book appeared greater attention would be directed towards Lew's poetry and that a larger audience and greater recognition of its merits would be his. Unfortunately, less than a month before the book was published, Lew, in a dark turn of mind, walked off into the woods of Nevada County to die.

He, more than many poets, would be very glad to know how much renewed life and strength is left in poetry in San Francisco, in the United States, and, believe it or not, the world.

22 Feb 75   — DM
Okie Hill

Golden Gate

Introduction

1. Brief Primer

America's speech waterfalls forth in meltingpot
tongues of Babel in
   telegraphic ads, pop songs, street-corner rapping,
bar room brag & bluster, bad-mouthing, put-ons, put-
downs,
   the home-made rhetorics of Whitman, Melville,
Andrew Jackson Davis, L. Ron Hubbard; the stream-
clear prose of Thoreau or Hemingway; Gertrude
Stein's devotions;
   the sportcaster's spiel tracing a horse race over &
thru the radio; the hawking, squawking, conning &
jiving; preaching, teaching, wheeling & dealing; the
jive-ass realms of speech; the hard-sell, the soft-soap-
ing;
   gossip columnists, breathless, telling-all; right-on;
telling It like It is; can you dig it? letting it all hang
out

anyway, it's all semantic;

hermetic trade lingo: jazz musicians, short-order cooks, truck-drivers, car mechanics, stereo buffs, do-it-yourself, tool talk—the technologic speech forms, machine-sprouted vocabularies whose sounds rebound in & out of USA livingrooms & bedrooms;

the self & tribe protective languages, shields against a rude deluge—layer & layer—worthless degrading words—

the black man's linguistic counter-attack on white America's word-gas clouds webbed with war-blood; the same cloud hanging over the American Indian (whose language was charged & precise as what a poet wants his to be), the Chicano, the Puerto Rican;

curt New England speech brittle as icicles; the Southerner's smoothing-out of word sounds; the Midwesterner's flat speech of plains; the shtetl-to-ghetto Yiddishisms of the Eastern cities; the regional, community, tribal tongues;

shop-talk, cop-talk, bop-talk, TV's hypno-rant; the daily dose of phony baloney; the nightly hot air;

animal invective clash of sounds as radical meets reactionary, as power crashes down on the powerless;

these sounds, the languages, these codes & messages, all meet in the ears & eyes of poets who have been Jacob-wrestling Europe since landing on Plymouth Rock.

America was claimed: a new place, a new space to build great cities on.

The poets began immediately to innocently & arrogantly fashion a language to meet & match America's impossible largeness.

Eldridge Cleaver calls USA Babylon because in the Bible Babylon was a dying city rotten with corruption, injustice & oppression. For the poet America is also

Babel with Babel's loud noise of voices trying to speak sense to each other. The air vibrates with the chaos of delusive and illusive language, hysteria, propaganda, the slick monotones of commerce—all out to net the mind, the soul. To snare it, bag it, cocoon its ability to function.

The poet's work is to activate the mind to its full measure of perception & receptivity. The poem is an event created from a fusion, a wedding of learned skills & unknown sources. After trying to get it all down—the faces, voices, dreams & fears—the poet begins to realize that all the voices are one & it is his work to make it heard.

It's all a flow of light, a following of light to light's source.

That's what poets do, what we all do, who are awake & resist the dark dead thought brings.

What makes a poet different is how he uses language in a way to penetrate you & how he listens to words & watches them move & what he sees & hears & how he puts it all together into a poem.

For many years on the back of *Poetry* (Chicago) there was a quote of Walt Whitman's. It said that good poems demand a good audience. Walt was right. Anyone who requires the language of poetry must be in the same constant training as a poet is. You must never take a poem for granted unless it's a bad one & then you should know why it's bad & how it could be better. The song in a poem isn't muzak, something in the background, a monotonous soundtrack to calm the stomach. The poem, as Whitman said, *demands* attention.

One's relation with the poem is one-to-one—as loving is.

It's that simple, it's that difficult; it is always worth the effort.

Poetry is the special use of language which weds invisible & visible worlds into words generating great power when chosen correctly.

A poem can be both an immediate & timeless source of information, revelation & pleasure. Poets use language with precision because they have learned respect for the mysteries inherent in words. The language of poetry is the language of discovery.

The poet can give you new sight, new insight. His poem provides passage through thoughts & perception in order for you to see thru the veils & know new meanings.

The poet is a revolutionary because he is constantly subverting corrupt institutional languages with his art. He can make the life-denying rhetoric of power politics void by singing one coherent, true song. The words connect in a man so that he stops & thinks.

"Oh, I never thought of it that way. I never saw it quite like that. Yes, now I see."

A poem can snap the lights on. That's how revolution begins.

2.

The six poets in this book represent the history of poetry in San Francisco, in America, in the world.

To be a poet in America & to survive is very difficult. The systems seem at odds with the artist & his ways of survival are few & often they break him into a life of ritualized compromise.

Poetry demands full-time workers as well as any other kind of work. It's unfair & uncaring to say that a poet who spends ten hours trying to get a poem right—a word, a line—isn't working as hard as a construction worker, a carpenter, a man unloading cargo on the docks.

The concept of work & work's yield finds it almost impossible to accept the work & the product a poet creates. It is a life's work our society places little value on. The poem does not have the same currency as a new car, the same built-in consumer need. A poem doesn't soothe class-agonies nor appease the poor as a color TV does.

When I recently applied for Welfare, the lady on the phone said, "Yes, I have an aunt who writes poems. Poetry is fine, but what do you DO?"

She'd been trained to know that being a poet wasn't a job. It was an anti-social act counting for almost nothing in a materialist society—unless, of course, I could convert (subvert) my word-facility ("Aptitude") into writing advertisements or cereal-box blurbs or best-sellers ("Go on, honey, go into your room & write a best-seller") or a hit-song—anything but writing poems ("They're okay to do if you got a regular job.") . . .

Education is vital to the life of poetry, yet poetry is usually taught in public schools as a dreaded chore—a gruesome effort memorizing Longfellow's doggerel kitsch, or the cruel fate of being forced to grapple with Coleridge's Ancient Mariner & feeling the squeeze of the old salt's albatross around your own neck.

We are, at the start, indoctrinated to the useless-ness of poetry. Thoughtless teaching makes its cadences un-natural to our ears—even though on the streets we'll dance & sing to game-chants & rhymes bouncing with the basics of poetry's components. It is a shame because nobody has more fun with language than kids. They delight in permutating words into sounds & rhythmical gobble; freely repeating words, singing wordless songs—yet as soon as they get into a classroom the joy of language is congealed into the grim business of drill-learning. Language becomes a serious matter & something you don't fool around with.

The poem is an experience that is concentrated in sounds, rhythms, primal symbols, turning the reader into the experience related, transforming him into the experiencer. It is a fusion, an entering into, an opening up—not a slamming of vault doors & the shutting-off of lights.

It's worthwhile noting that all of the six poets are also teachers, either on the platform or in the classroom, & most of them have taught poetry to college-level students. It is a loss to the art that more poets don't teach grade-schoolers. It would be, I'm sure, a tremendous exchange of learnings. Each could teach the other many old & new tricks.

Somehow or other, poets survive, & to survive as a poet in America—to survive intact—takes toughness, imagination & a gritty flexible intelligence.

Is it any wonder that the poets who do survive are considered by many to be dangerous?

These six poets are survivors. They are tough, yet tender, loving men. Their knowledge is complex & goes deep, yet their purpose as poets is to transmit it to you.

A poet learns, teaches, tries to keep the wisdoms alive inside, passing them on in works made up out of the best cominations of what he knows.

A poet comes to his tribe with song & if the song is

good, if the words work & sound right together, the tribe is renewed, restored &, for a moment united & free.

3. Work Song: More Notes

This book took a lot of time to put together & there were many people who helped out, who put in their own time, sympathy & ideas during its creation. There's no correct way to truly thank these people who helped me with this strange task.

Jack Shoemaker, first of all, helped beyond measure. He provided transportation, since I don't drive, into the city, & was an important voice in many of the interviews. (The initials "JS" in an interview means that Jack is talking, asking a thoughtful question.) His encouragement, his useful ideas, helped direct the book's outcome as much as anything.

Liz Pintchuck toiled more than anybody else & worked out of the goodness of her heart—certainly not for the criminally meagre money offered her. Poor Liz had to transcribe the interviews, usually poorly recorded, onto paper using a clumsy plastic portable typewriter. We did not have access to more sophisticated & time-saving tools as electric typewriters, tape-pedals, &tc. (In fact putting this all together often took the hysterical form of a demon opera. Poet Vs. Machine. Faulty tape-recorders, car breakdown, power failures . . . &tc.)

Liz would transcribe the interview tape & send the rough transcript to me & I would then revise the transcript & tape my revision & send the tape to Liz & she, in turn, would type it out & send the revised typescript back to me. I would correct it &—yes, you are ahead of me!—she would then type the final typescript & mail it back to me. It seemed like an endless job for her, like something you might encounter only in a nightmare. But Liz endured it all with humor & grace. Bless you.

My wife Tina paid her dues listening to me rage & holler when things went wrong, snarled & tangled, & she also patiently went over the final draft for last minute corrections & proof-reading.

Thanks are also due to Bob Briggs of Dial-Delacorte who introduced me to George Young, then Ballantine's West Coast editor, who thought this would be a good idea for a book.

Final thanks go to the six poets who were gracious, always helpful, & who endured our machinery, our questions & occasional lack of tact. They maintained their good natures, offered their hospitality, & wished me well. I hope they are pleased with this book. It is hard to trap a moment. Poets know this all too well.

DAVID MELTZER
Mill Valley, 1970

Kenneth Rexroth

1

KR: I came to California in 1927 to live. The day I got into town, San Francisco's leading poet, California's leading poet, killed himself. George Sterling. He pretty well represented the California scene in those days which lived on its past. The San Francisco literary world was dominated by people to whom the native son and daughter thing was all important, although most of them were not native sons and daughters. I don't think Gertrude Atherton, George Sterling, any of these people, were born in California.

It's hard to believe now, with all the tremendous activity that has been in San Francisco, that San Francisco, when we came there to live, was very much of a backwater town and there just wasn't anything happening. There was this myth of Carmel which is just like it is now . . . like the myth of Big Sur . . . and a lot of those people are still alive down there . . . they stagger, run around juiced, and bellow out folk songs.

That's really the reason we stayed here, as it was a

long way from the literary marketplace. We didn't know anybody who wasted his time talking about what Horace Gregory thought of Oscar Williams. We met people who would say to you, "Who do you think is California's leading writer?" And you would say, "Gertrude Stein." They would say, "Who is that?" And then they would say, "Oh, yes!" They knew her, you see, her brother was in society on the Peninsula, but they didn't know she wrote. It was a very strange scene. It's like Santa Barbara now. It was a little time pocket.

DM: What was Robinson Jeffers' effect on the California scene at that time?

KR: Jeffers wasn't very well known in California then. He was just beginning to acquire a reputation among a very limited number of people. The people who dominated the literary scene in California looked down on him. They viewed him as being terribly modernistic.

We just didn't have any competition. It was like Picasso dropping back into the world of Trollope. The leading painter in town, Maynard Dixon, came over to see me and looked at my paintings on the wall and said, "Hmmmm, I see you have been experimentin' with abstract form, like Matissy and Picassio!" So, it was a great place, you know, because there wasn't any sweat. That's why we came to San Francisco.

DM: Was it in the thirties that the California poets and artists became more involved with the world and with each other's works?

KR: I don't think there were very many people in the thirties. There were people in San Francisco who were writing and not publishing anything when I came. Most of those people became involved in red San Francisco. The interesting thing is that most of them became practical labor organizers, rather than Bohemians sitting around in Union Square arguing about proletarian literature.

There was a real pattern there, due to the fact that there were all sorts of things wrong with red literature in the thirties in New York. But when the Communist artist and writer's groups were formed, the John Reed Club . . . the one in San Francisco, they put up some pretty stiff qualifications. The members were actually artists and writers. They stayed around.

What happened in New York was that the clubs became dominated by Bohemians who didn't do anything except argue about Marx, whom they had never read, and they would avoid the artists and writers. It's very hard to convey to the present generation what that was like. People talked about communism in those days the way people talk about acid or smack. I mean, they bored you to death, and they didn't know anything about it.

I was sort of the outdoor organizer for the John Reed Club. I was organizer of everything in the West, and, of course, the New York apparatus thought the West started at Hoboken and that is one reason the Chicago organization was better—the reason it had people like Dick Wright and Farrell and people like that. Outside of New York, we tried to confine the thing to bona fide artists and writers. In San Francisco our people were actually involved in the real labor movement. You have to understand that there was an enormous amount of bullshit. People were running around talking about "the masses" and there wasn't really any contact with the masses. But hell, I mean, I wrote the *Waterfront Worker* . . . all of the goddamn thing, week after week after week. A mimeographed thing we used to hand out on the waterfront long before the strike. All of us were actually involved. We were involved in the Agricultural Workers Industrial Union. I had somebody ask me one time at an anarchist meeting in Italy, "Is *The Grapes of Wrath* true?" One-eighth is true. In the novel, one guy gets killed. In a Bakersfield cotton strike, to which I took Steinbeck, eight guys get killed.

You see, all of us were very actively involved and this makes all the difference in the world. Another thing, very few of these people were orthodox Commies because the basic tradition on the West Coast was IWW. The attitude was really an anarchistic attitude, and for many years I treasured—to flaunt in the face of the FBI, if they ever bothered me—an application to the Communist Party that had written across it, "Comrade Rexroth is a very valuable comrade, but he is entirely too much of an anarchist to be good party material." It was signed by Earl Browder, the general secretary of the Party. This movement stretched all the way from Seattle, where the IWW dominated the intellectual and Bohemian world in the years around the First World War and well into the twenties. People like Gary Snyder, over a generation later than myself, and I grew up in very similar worlds.

The first time I met Gary Snyder, he hitchhiked down and stayed at the house. He was on his way from Reed College, and I said, "Gee, you're tan, what have you been doing?" And he said, "I have been working on a lookout outside of Marble Mount on the Sagit River in the Mount Baker forest." And I said, "I used to work up there. I was a patrolman before they had lookouts. . . . The guy I worked for just got the job. He was a wonderful district ranger, his name was Tommy Thompson." And Gary gave me a kind of funny look and he said, "Well, that's who I was working for this year. It is his last year and he is retiring."

Of course, there is another thing, people on the West Coast work. Ginsberg when he came out here, as he said in interviews, was working as a market researcher, which is just a shit job. It's like being a floorwalker in a dime store. I said, "Why don't you

work? How much are you making? Forty-five dollars?
You can't live on forty-five dollars in San Francisco.
That's not money. Why don't you go to work, get a
job?" Ginsberg said, "What do you mean?" And I
said, "Ship out. Do you realize that when they go
into the Bering Sea, you are in hot water? And you
know what that means? That means double pay.
You come back with more bread than you know
what to do with!" I don't know how many trips Allen
made in the next couple of years. In the East people
don't think like that. We were talking earlier about
Hart Crane. He spent all his time fretting about his
economic problems, but if he had been a Westerner,
he would have gone out and gotten a job in the woods
or at sea, or something like that and he would have
made a lot of bread. A hell of a lot more bread than
he ever did writing advertising copy for candy.

There's another thing that I would like to point out,
and that is that there has been right along in San
Francisco a pretty consistent, relentless organizational
activity. At the time of the Moscow trials and the
general bankruptcy of orthodox Bolshevism, relatively
few people in San Francisco became Trotskyites. The
people who did were pumped in from New York and
were connected with the Sailors Union of the Pacific.
Most people just backed away and went back to what
they were before. All during those years we always
had poetry readings and discussions and then during
the war we set up a thing called the Randolph Bourne
Council in which we gathered up the radical intellectuals in town that were not Stalinist. We tried to
gather the Trotskyites, which was hopeless. Immediately after the war we simply organized an open and
aboveboard Anarchist Circle. We used to have bigger
meetings than any other radical group. All of these
people, my generation and slightly younger, were
involved in it, they all came . . . Bob Stock and a
couple of other people who were in the group had

poetry readings too on another day in the week . . .
all closely tied with the Libertarian Circle. The whole
purpose of the Libertarian Circle was to reevaluate
and refound the movement. You have no idea of the
degree to which orthodox Bolshevism had completely
conditioned the minds of the generality of intellectuals in those days. We used to shock people because
we used to say, "We don't proselytize, we don't have
any agenda, we don't have any chairman." There
were two hundred people and there was no chairman
and it was all very orderly. It was necessary to work
out these techniques of group relationships, techniques of discussion which you might call a new kind
of dialectic, and then information . . . week after
week after week people led discussions, people would
volunteer to speak about libertarian literature, education, agriculture, everything under the sun. It was
a long process of education for the whole generation
of people. These people are now between forty and
fifty. We had all kinds of college students . . . all of
the San Francisco poets of that period, lots of writers
. . . people who became psychiatrists, people who became college professors, people who became engineers, they are all still around.

Out of the group came KPFA. Lou Hill was a member of our group as well as most of the people who
were the original KPFA staff. The station was devoted to the reeducation of its audience on what you
might call libertarian principles. There was a constant dose of poetry, for instance. Later they all began
fighting with one another and became impoverished.
They cannibalized an immense library of tapes. The
first tapes Dylan Thomas ever made . . . I was in
England immediately after the war and taped readings and interviews and sent them back to San Francisco. These things were priceless. David Gascoyne,
Dylan, Henry Treece, Alex Comfort, Herbert Read,

and George Woodcock . . . discussions with the whole English anarchist circle.

We kept pumping in stuff from all over, in German, in English, in French . . . I sat up night after night after night writing letters abroad and this material just flooded in and it didn't go to New York. I was corresponding with Simone Weil, Camus, before the *Partisan Review* ever heard of them! Later they were turned up for New York by Dwight and Nancy MacDonald. The person in New York who dug this thing at all was Dwight MacDonald with his magazine *Politics* . . . to which none of us would contribute. This annoyed Dwight very much!

We set up a thing in San Francisco in the thirties called the Artists' and Writers' Union which generated a strong tradition. People who are that old remember it with great fondness. The members were all highly qualified artists and writers. Then the WPA came along. We had certain contacts in Washington, and we knew this was going to happen, so we were ready to capitalize on it. Before they ever set up the WPA, when Roosevelt first came in, they started shoveling out money to relieve the crisis. They set up a thing called the Public Works of Art Projects, and I got a telephone call in the middle of the night from Washington and I was told that they were going to set it up. So when the director of the De Young Museum, and a rich patron, and our big rich commercial artist met for their preliminary meeting, there were about two hundred and fifty people in the court of the De Young Museum, notified overnight! And they were all bona fide artists. We just took over.

We decorated Coit Tower. It looks like the Diego Rivera funny papers, but it was a very great achievement. Nobody else in the country did a goddamn thing except take government checks. An awful lot of stuff was definitely accomplished. No other WPA program later put out anything like those magazines we put out . . . and we were responsible for a book, *American Stuff*. We got creative projects set up. There were all kinds of people who we told, "Here is your check, go home and write." Eventually we got people on creative writing projects all around the country. People wrote books of poems, novels, and some got themselves Ph.D.s, but of course all of this had to be done quietly because of congressional criticism. But a tremendous amount was accomplished. Between 1950 and 1955, the necessity for organization began to die out because other people could become activist. It was no longer necessary to educate somebody to make an anarchist poet out of him. He had a milieu in which he could naturally become such a thing. But for years, it was a slow process of breaking down rigid ideologies and then creating a different thing.

2

KR: The Vietnam war was a disaster because until the Vietnam war got hot, the dominant tendency in the movement in America was anarchist-pacifist . . . and religious in various ways. What happened with Vietnam, and the Russian-Chinese split, was that the movement again fell into the hands of people who were representing other people's foreign offices. American radicals are placed in the ridiculous position of supporting the foreign policies of Ho Chi Minh, or Chairman Mao, or Fidel Castro, of Tito, or Israel. That may be better than Stalin, but it is still an army, it is still a foreign office, it is still a state, and I think that were we let alone, and the Vietnam war ended, this would die out. You see the Vietnam war gives . . . in the strict sense of the word . . . a political complexion to the movement which it had almost got rid of.

Today so much in the movement is dominated by state-ism. What is Israel? Israel is another bourgeois state. Not only that, but it is a theocracy. You walk up and down the streets of Tel Aviv publicly eating a pork chop sandwich and find out what happens to you. You know! Here's a Negro in San Francisco and he is running around in African clothes and he's talking about the glories of the Congo or Nigeria or Ghana or whatever side he has taken. Why? What for? It is just another state. It is the same old shit come back, as Marx said. This doesn't mean that I am supporting the Vietnam war, or that I am pro-imperialist, pro-Arab . . . but with all this national tension there has been a recrudescence of state-ism in the American movement, but it is only the leadership. Students don't have this attitude. For students it's all a lot of crap, except for a few blacks who just discovered it—who just read Fanon.

The students participate in issues that involve them. They participate in an anti-Vietnam demonstration because they are going to be asked to murder and they are going to be murdered. They participate in actions against the deadly system of the university which is designed to turn them into murderers. The objection to the Vietnam war on the part of students is an organic objection. I have never been able to understand why anybody went to war. I look at a guy marching down the street in uniform and I can't understand it. I can't understand anybody doing that. Somebody comes around to me and says, "I could never face my mother, my family, the social pressures . . ."

I once spent the day with a leading Comintern representative in Hollywood, a wealthy movie actor, and a couple of sophisticated top Communists in the movie star's yacht arguing with Eisenstein, trying to persuade him to stay in America. Any movie company would have given him anything, anything! I'll never forget it. We all got sunburned as hell and the argument was just hopeless.

He said, "No." The Russians told him that if he defected they would expose him as a homosexual. And somebody on the yacht said "Well, so what?" And Eisenstein said, "It would kill my mother." So he went back to Russia and Stalin destroyed him . . . artistically. I never really understand people who yield to pressures like that.

I don't understand anybody who goes into the army. Who in the hell wants to go into the army and shoot anybody? I just can't conceive of it for any reason. I mean, any prison is better than the army . . . any prison. So when a movement objects to a war, the rank and file, whatever their leaders represent, the rank and file have a perfectly natural organic objection.

The university is set up today, and is set up for no other purpose, to provide bureaucrats for the military-industrial complex and to hold bodies in cold storage —off the labor market. It is set up for nothing else.

The students object to this because it is soul-destroying. The human relationships in a university today are soul-destroying. The fabric is soul-destroying. The way the classroom is set up with that one-armed crippled furniture, like an old-time cafeteria . . . the way you can't turn around to look at somebody; the way you have to face the boss on a podium. When I go into one of my seminars, I break this up completely. We sit on the floor. We get a room where we can move the furniture out of the way. I sit in the back amongst the people. Or we sit in a circle. The university is not unique, there is built into all society today actual physical soul-destroying structures. Did you ever take a chick into a motel in southern California? It has a fucking machine in it. The bed fucks. You put a quarter in it and the bed fucks. You don't have to do any work. Right here in Santa Barbara, within walking distance, is a motel and every bed has a fucking machine in it. This is not a joke, this is true. They say it is a Relaxicisor, a Jacuzzi or something . . . but that's what it's for.

The whole civilization is like this, so that the revolt of the movement, young and old, is against the destruction of the human race. All these people come around, yellow, black, and Latin American, and say, "Oh, man, all you have to do is just to follow our boss and do what the state tells you to do. Go to Israel and live in a kibbutz and all your problems will be solved." That's a lot of crap. They're not solved at all, as is self-evident from Czechoslovakia, or the relation between Russia and China . . .

I have complete sympathy with the movement but I no longer belong to anything. (I guess I belong to Resist. I think I signed something and sent them some money, because its purpose is the oldies to help the youngies. And the leadership . . . people like Chomsky, Reisman, and Fromm . . . I look on these people as considerably to the right of myself . . . of course, Chomsky is changing.) I think it's a disaster that this new wave of revolutionary nationalism has become reflected in the American movement with which it has nothing to do.

DM: In a sense, though, this is a reflection of the powers that they are in resistance to. This happens often, don't you think so?

KR: Sure. What do you think would happen to you if

you marched down the streets of Peking with a banner saying: "Free Grass, Free Huey, Free Love"? . . . Oh shit! [*Laughter.*] All these regimes are extremely puritanical and their art is . . . did you ever read *Chinese Literature*, the magazine they put out? It's just appalling.

DM: As bad as reading *Soviet Literature*?

KR: That's Gertrude Stein and James Joyce compared with the stuff that comes from China.

DM: What about the radical art of today? Do you see anything beyond propaganda in the poetry and in the fiction?

KR: Fiction, you know, is like painting. It's become so commercialized that it destroys the people who create it. Mitch Goodman, in a number of *Liberation*, talks about Mailer. He says what everybody knows about Mailer. He criticizes Mailer for the long attack on Paul Goodman, which I thought was simply scandalous. The reason that a guy like Mailer comes into existence is that there was this young radical kid running around Okinawa, or Guadalcanal, or some place jumping from foxhole to foxhole, and jumping beyond him is a publisher's scout, or an agent with a checkbook and a contract. Look, the first American antiwar novel was John Dos Passos' *Three Soldiers*. It came out in the middle twenties. These other guys were brought up right away to give them something really antiwar . . . but they got all the gold when they were twenty years old and haven't been a damn bit of good since. The same is true of painting. Painting has become incredibly commercialized. If a Buick agency was run with the ruthless commercialism of a modern art gallery, it would go out of business. It would be just too commercial. You have to be just a little human to sell Buicks.

And poetry . . . book poetry in bulk has come to be dominated by the professor-poet. Publishing a book of poetry is part of the publish-or-perish setup. You go to any university today and you are up to your ass in poets.

I get this stuff that comes to me for review. People say, "Why don't you review it?" I can't read through any of it because it is toilet-paper poetry. Every sheet looks just like every other sheet. It's fantastic.

In the McCarthy period when the only expression of any kind of radicalism was confined to science fiction, I used to review science fiction for KPFA. I sat around one night making a tape for them. I had a bunch of science fiction books stacked up before me . . . you read them, you know, zippp! Just like that! I'd put the unread ones in one pile and read them and put them in another pile, and I went to take a piss and returned and picked up a new book, read it, and Christ! I get fifty pages into it and realized, Gee, have I started on the wrong pile? I have already read that!

Well, the poetry is the same way. You know where the poetry is. The poetry is in song. The poetry is in direct relationship. The poetry is the kind of thing existing in San Francisco, that continuous human contact. At one time just the Libertarian Circle, and Bob Stock's basement and now . . . God knows how many . . . there must be a hundred poetry readings a night in the damn city, in crash pads, in coffee shops, everyplace under the sun.

A person like Leonard Cohen, for instance, was getting nowhere with the literary establishment. You had to go to Canada to even hear of Leonard Cohen. But the minute Leonard started singing, he went like wildfire all over the USA. He can't sing. So much the better. (This is something you run into all the time. People are always saying, for instance: Dylan is terrible, he can't sing . . .) Leonard Cohen can't sing but that's part of the thing, and they don't understand this. The thing that makes Leonard Cohen what he is, is that he doesn't give a fuck whether he sings or not. I mean, he is communicating . . . he's in direct communication with people, which is one of the reasons, of course, that he opts out of show business.

You know what happened last year . . . he had a tour set up and he started out on it and soon he said, "To hell with it, I'm going back to the Greek isles." He had lost human contact. This is where poetry is. The poetry here is in the same place that it is in France. The greatest postwar French poet is George Brassens . . . the poet-singer. It sure as hell isn't Yves Bonnefoy, who is a kind of bad combination of Yvor Winters and H.D. Jesus Christ, what good was two thousand years of civilization to produce that!

Now there are hundreds of people and they are all over the map. There are a few great ones. People like Anne Sylvestre . . . incidentally, all the young singers and poets are anarchist. Listen to their records, they make all sorts of sly digs at Leo Ferré, Louis Aragon, and the old guard. From the days of Appollinaire to the present, the leading French poets worth their salt all wrote for direct presentation; the modern tradition goes back to the nineteenth century to Charles Cros and Aristide Bruant and continues to the middle ages. That is why I am so interested in the stuff that you do, because you are the only one of the San Francisco group who has really made a very professional thing out of this, nobody else has. I would if I had the time, but I am getting old and have just so much time to do what I have to do.

Back in the days of poetry and jazz, Ferlinghetti, Patchen, and myself all were well aware of this. The essence of the thing was in the direct speech of one person to another. Since none of us were singers, we read. Also there were other reasons for that. It gave a jazz musician much greater freedom. And poets were a hell of a lot easier to get along with! Just talk to a jazz musician and ask him what he thinks of a singer.

DM: Would it be possible to talk about the poetry and jazz? For instance, when did you actually begin experimenting with it?

KR: When I was a young kid in my teens. I ran a place in Chicago, with a couple of girls, called the Green Mask. We used to have poetry readings there all the time. The girls were a couple of carny and show business women, and the Green Mask was a hangout for show business people. One of those old-time places where everybody goes after the show, where people get up and sing. Maxwell Bodenheim (who couldn't write for sour owlshit) and Langston Hughes and myself used to do poetry and jazz with a Chicago group, the Austin High Gang.

Dave Tough was the youngest member of the group and was himself a poet. Dave Tough was just about the first hipster. He was a head, and most of the time lived with gay women and he wrote poetry—real far-out poetry. There was another drummer, whose name I forget, who lives in Florida now, who has Dave's poetry. I have tried to get at it. I turned Barney Rosset onto it, but I don't know what happened. It wasn't amateur illiterate stuff. Dave Tough was, of course, the greatest organic drummer . . . the only musician, except Mary Lou Williams, who went from the old-time jazz to the new-time jazz. Nobody else did.

DM: I remember hearing Pee Wee Russell playing *Blue Monk* recently . . .

KR: Yeah, but played in that strange Pee Wee way. I mean, the thing about Dave Tough is that he moved from Chicago jazz into modern jazz. He was in the first Herd with Woody Herman, for instance, and through it all became a thoroughly modern drummer. He was certainly as interesting as Roach or even Elvin Jones.

Later in the John Reed Club we used to do a certain amount of revolutionary verse. I did a thing with Louis Aragon's *Red Front* . . . and then it all sorta died. Jazz died. There was very little action in jazz for years.

See, the great problem, is that to do a thing really well in the first place, the poet has to know a great deal about music, either play an instrument or be able to write music or both. He should have some idea about what is happening. Then the band has to rehearse. You don't just get up and blow. And if you lived in San Francisco, the better bands were not available because they were on tour. The musicians were moving around all the time. That's why we started in The Cellar, because the owners were the band. The piano player (Bill Weisjahn) and the drummer (Sonny Wayne) were the owners. And Bruce Lippincott on tenor . . . they were the house band. Other musicians came and went and played with the band. (Mingus and I did something a long time ago in The Black Cat during the war, just for fun one night.) As soon as Ferlinghetti did it, then Patchen brought out his record with a highly trained group. Mingus and Langston Hughes played the Five Spot in New York after I did, and I understand it was very successful.

Two things happened during the Beat Generation time. The hucksters couldn't understand it at all. I remember having a conference with a record company, with Laughlin and the New Directions people, about marketing Patchen's record. The executives of the company didn't know what they had at all. They didn't know how to sell it. The only thing that was selling at all was this Ken Nordine record . . . which was to us what Rod McKuen is to Ginsberg. A strictly commercial scene.

Steve Allen got that same idea. I don't know how

he formed his friendship with Kerouac. I was booked
into the Village Vanguard and Kerouac recruited the
gig. They throw you out of the Musicians' Union for
doing something like that, but he went to Max Gor-
don and recruited the gig. He said it would help build
up my show. Well he was pissyass drunk every night,
vomited on the piano, and made a general ass of
himself, and Max said to me, "Look, I'll buy your
contract." Steve was very upset. I said no to Max.
(Max started out in life as an anarchist poet, very
few people know that.) Well, this started a thing so
that in every Greenwich Village coffee shop and bar
for about two years, all kinds of bums with pawn-
shop saxophones put together with scotch tape, and
some other guy with something called poetry, were,
like, you know, blowing poetry, man, dig? And it was
absolutely unmitigated crap. It killed the whole thing.
It had a terribly bad effect. There wasn't anything like
it in San Francisco because we had done the thing in
San Francisco . . . People knew it, people knew all
about it, even though there was an awful lot of trash
at the Coffee Gallery, but by and large the music was
better and the poetry was better too. But the stuff in
New York was ridiculous, and of course it's that whole
New York commercial scene. That was all it was for.
To make the tourist go to Greenwich Village. You
went down there where the first miniskirts were
worn, and the miniskirted chicks were waitresses,
and you got yourself a free grope, and you listened to
free jazz and poetry done by a couple of stumble-
bums who weren't being paid anything, and it killed
the whole thing. Then Lipton in Southern California
staged the first big show. It was very successful,
Shorty Rogers heading one group with me and
Freddy Katz heading the other. Lipton, Stu Perkoff,
and some others. This was quite a show. And it ran
for weeks and drew all kinds of people and made all
kinds of bread. The musicians were top musicians.

I was always luckier than anybody else because I knew more about what I was doing. I got top musicians. The people I had working with me at the Five Spot were part of the Blakey organization: Bobby Timmons, Doug Watkins, and the star of those days, Donald Byrd, and Elvin Jones on drums, and then Pepper Adams on baritone. The same in Chicago. The band I worked with up and down the coast was built around Brew Moore, who was a Lester Young-type tenor. He was very good for Kansas City soul. An awful lot of work went into this, long rehearsals. I always worked with head-arrangements. Patchen worked with stuff that was all written down.

But you discover that jazz audiences don't know shit from wild honey . . . and that includes a lot of the musicians. One of the things that I did, and still do, is done against Eric Satie's *Gymnopédie No. 1*. It is called *This Night Only*. People always think it is a George Shearing number. I used to do a thing with a Neruda poem to a 12/8 samba rhythm. I remember sitting down with two of the leading New York critics who were supposed to know something about music, who write about pop culture, jazz, and stuff like that . . . and they said, "Kenneth, why you know, that boogie-woogie number you did was very good."

The interesting thing was that they didn't know what 12/8 was, but they dug the 12/8 which was the essence of Jimmy Yancey, of boogie-woogie. Yet they didn't know it was Latin music. Dig? They were jazz habitués. In the Five Spot at least one night a week. That's one of the things that's heartbreaking about jazz.

Today you have a highly trained audience which has grown up listening to, you name it, Judy Collins, Joan Baez, Pete Seeger. They have good taste in rock, which is why they put down most rock now because

it has been debauched. You have a trained audience
which you did not have in the day of bop.

People still say the most absurd things. "You know,
that Charlie Parker is polyrhythmic and atonal." Oh,
my ass! I mean, there isn't anything in Charlie
Parker that isn't in Beethoven!

DM: They have reissued tapes of Parker playing in
nightclubs and often the audience chattering is
louder than the music . . .

KR: Of course, that's another thing. You play in New
York and you discover what hard bop really is. Hard
bop is music for people who don't listen. I would
never put up with it. In the first place, I have a lot of
projection and I won't permit any nonsense. I'll just
stop in the middle of a poem . . . but the minute I
got off the stage and the band took over, everybody
would start talking again. It was scandalous! Beautiful musicians like Watkins and Timmons, you know,
young guys . . . no wonder they never got anyplace.
Well, shit, I can see why. Bobby would play a solo
piano number and these motherfuckers would be
talking at the top of their lungs. Cash register-bang-
ing, waitress clinking around . . . that's what I
always loved about John Lewis. "The waitresses don't
hustle drinks during the set, the phone doesn't ring,
and take the bell off the cash register." Boy, that's
really twisting the arm of the owner! But Lewis and
Mingus are the only people . . . Lewis, of course, was
polite whereas Mingus was rough. But John is the
only person who has been able to get away with demands like that when his group performs at clubs.

DM: I get the feeling that jazz today is even more
neglected than at that time . . .

KR: Neglect? It's lost connection, partly because it's
so blatantly lowbrow and partly because it's so crazy
racist. And its racism really doesn't have anything to

do with black or white, it's just that there are too many pigs at the trough . . .

The black dominance of jazz is due to the fact that there just aren't enough gigs to go around. Blacks have got their leverage and they levered other people out. This is all tied in with Bohemian black negritude which has divorced them from their sources. Folks don't buy this. This whole Ayler, Leroi Jones scene cuts them off from folks, from black people, so that they lose their roots. Their white audience will only take so much of it and then they get bored. People get tired of being told musically, "You motherfucker, you kept me in slavery for three hundred years." The average guy in the audience didn't, he came over here to escape Hitler or Pilsudski. Then they discover that and they say, "You dirty Jew!" The audience gets tired of this after a while. Masochism is only fun for a little while. That's been a big factor.

Also the fact that they won't get away from these songs which provide them with certain kinds of changes which they can work on, but the lyrics of which are absurd. Look at all the jazz standards and then think of the words to them. There has been a demand, you see, for lyrics of a counterculture. I mean, jazz really wasn't enough of a counterculture, because jazz really isn't . . . jazz was, after all, music played for dance halls and cabarets and anybody who says it isn't is crazy. It's not the voice of a counterculture that most radical rock is.

I mean, you couldn't get out of the Sunset Cafe for less than thirty dollars. It cost you more than that to go to the Cotton Club. Langston Hughes said a wonderful thing about the Cotton Club. "You know, they didn't let in common niggers like me. It was for people like Bojangles Robinson." That isn't quite true, because I went to the Cotton Club with Langston . . . but it is roughly true. Above it all, like God in his heaven, was Duke. It was disgraceful, you know. The show would just make you vomit. Talk about Tom minstrel shows . . . these spade chicks walking around pretending to be cannibals . . . it was just terrible! No wonder Duke is so imperturbable. He would die of shame otherwise—not for himself, because his music is magnificent, but the whole atmosphere of the Cotton Club was horrible.

The thing in music that has happened in the last ten years is not as assimilable.

There's a lot of stuff that's assimilable and the square can't tell the difference. *Time* magazine is always discovering some new rock group offering wonderful lyrics about I-love-America, sung by people that look like Norman Rockwell Coca-Cola ads—but it doesn't go. Neither does the phony acid rock go. The audience won't take it.

I went to the Both/And Club one day to hear Philly Joe Jones. Philly Joe Jones is a great drummer. He's another organic drummer like Dave Tough. It's like a heartbeat, you know. It doesn't have to be loud. I mean, he could make a great thing with just one brush. And everybody in the audience was gray-haired. It was very funny. I said to the owners, "God, it's old home week!" And the owners said, "Yeah, it sure is. I don't know. Changes have been taking place, you know. I feel like we are booking Bix Beiderbeck."

Students of mine, even Negro students who really dig jazz, stop with Ornette and Mingus and maybe three or four other musicians. This savage hard bop, I mean postbop, that has come up in the last couple of years in New York . . . civilization is breaking down. Don't forget that jazz musicians work for a living, they have to work in clubs and they are not living off in communes. If you play a guitar you can say, fuck it, and walk out under a redwood tree. But jazz musicians are tied into a very fierce and ugly scene which is controlled by the Mafia. . . . What

kind of a world is this to work in? A modern folk
singer or a modern rock musician doesn't have to do
that at all . . . he is not tied into the gangster world. . . .

3

DM: There is a seemingly different response to spiritual matters in the West Coast; a type of life-style and
response more basically rooted to oriental and pre-
institutionalized Judeo-Christian concepts . . .
KR: One reason is simply that oceans, like the
steppes, unite as well as separate. The West Coast is
close to the Orient. It's the next thing out there.
There are a large number of orientals living on the
West Coast. San Francisco is an international city
and it has living contact with the Orient. It also has
an internal oriental life. Once a week you can go to
see a Buddhist basketball game if you want to. There
are Buddhist temples all over the place. To a New
Yorker this is all ridiculous, the Orient means dime-
store incense burners. It is very unreal.

For years I noticed in Pound's "Cantos" two ideo-
grams that were upside-down. I used to pester
Laughlin about this. I used to make fun of it. Ezra
by this time had gotten very dim-witted, so he didn't
notice it. This was after the war. . . . Laughlin said
something to Eliot about it, and Eliot burst out laugh-
ing and thought it was a great joke. Not that they

were upside-down, but that it would worry me. He
said, "But, you know, no one pays any attention at
all to that sort of stuff. You know, that Chinese thing.
Nobody reads Chinese anyway." Eliot's attitude
toward Ezra's interest in the Orient was that it was a
great deal more ridiculous than his interest in social
credit, or his other crackpot ideas.

Large numbers of people have gone to the Northwest and to California to get away from the extreme
pressures of a commercial civilization. On the West
Coast it is possible to beat the system. It's possible
to be a fly alive on the flywheel, which it isn't in New
York. I would have been an utterly different human
being if I had gone back to New York. That's why I
stayed on the West Coast. Of course, there is another
aspect to the whole California business: religious
communities and new religions and swamis, you
know, maybe that's just because of a large number
of middle-aged women. You know what they call those
swamis in old-time show business? They called them
"ragheads on the menopause circuit." But, at the
same time, a guy like Krishnamurti, who certainly
plays the menopause circuit, not out of his own
wishes . . . I mean he doesn't ask for it, they come
to him . . . Krishnamurti is a very impressive guy.
His stuff is very intelligent. He is no Kahlil Gibran.
He has wonderful answers to give.

This is all part of the wartime thing too. Allen
Hunter at the Hollywood Congregational Church is
the guy who turned on people like Auden, Aldous
Huxley, Pravananda, Gerald Heard, and of course,
Isherwood, who is still around. All of these people
were extremely influential on the pacifist and anarchist movements. This was another focus. And it all
fed into the thing that made the San Francisco scene.

People would come down from the CO camps to

us in San Francisco, but they would also go down to see Isherwood, or Aldous Huxley, or somebody like that. Something definitely was being built up.

The big influences in the Northwest were Mark Tobey, who was a Bahai, and Morris Graves, who was a Vedantist. They were both very serious about it. Mark Tobey is a big wheel in the Bahai movement, in so far as they have big wheels. And Morris Graves is very serious. A lot of western migration was in the first place to get away from the destructiveness of the big metropoles and then to find new spiritual roots. That's true of all classes of people, not just intellectuals.

I think it's a great mistake to put down the thought of an old retired couple in Moline, Illinois, who decide to get themselves a little house in the rose-colored slums of southern California after going to a Vedanta meeting. There's nothing wrong with that. The guy comes home and says, "Ma, I think I am going to sell the secondhand car business. I think it is a rotten thing. I think we got enough money and we will go to California. I was sure impressed by that Indian fella we heard at that lecture and I think we'll go out to Glendale . . ." What's wrong with this? Is it any different than Allen Ginsberg?

I have always said that the greatest shock Kerouac ever got in his life was when he walked into my house, sat down in a kind of stiff-legged imitation of a lotus posture, and announced he was a Zen Buddhist . . . and then discovered everyone in the room knew at least one Oriental language.

You have to realize too that KPFA fed us an awful lot of this stuff. For years and years, Alan Watts and I were back-to-back on Sunday. Alan was handing out the Sunday sermon. This was all very influential. The very name, "Pacifica Views," Jimmy Broughton's brother was, I think, the financier of it. There are lots of connections here that go back to the war years.

Then too, consider the large numbers of conscientious objectors who made up the movement in San Francisco. Most of them were real young kids who just didn't know any better, and they went on doing what their Sunday School superintendent told them to do after he stopped telling them what to do. They found themselves out here in concentration camps. They had no roots, no background at all. They didn't really understand what had happened to them. And they began to put together a thing. Look at the tremendous Catholic, pacifist, anarchist movement that exists today. Well, Christ, the San Francisco Fellowship of Reconciliation assumed the responsibility of feeding the Catholics in CO camps. It was impossible to do it. They damn near starved to death. I can remember when the Catholic Worker group numbered in the whole USA about two hundred people. Lots of those people came to the Bay Area and settled here. Today, it's an enormous movement all over the world. It's now universal. Civilization is in a state of total collapse. We live in a corpse, and more and more people know this and seek for a way out . . .

An awful lot of these people stopped writing, or write very little. There was a whole group of people around Berkeley those days who were not part of Bob's Berkeley Rennaissance and were members of the San Francisco circle. They are still around but most of them are not writing. One, of course, who is still writing is Philip Lamantia.

He has an incomparable European reputation but is not well known in America. Of course, the thing about Philip is that he doesn't promote himself at all. I mean, not at all. And he is always away. You know, he is off someplace. He is in Mexico, or he is in Tangiers, or he is in Spain, Paris, and he is ignored by the American avant-garde establishment. Yet everybody knows . . . you ask Ferlinghetti, or Duncan, or somebody like that, and they all acknowledge

Lamantia's importance—but he is not around when the prizes are awarded. And, of course, Philip represents as all of us represent something that for many years has been an absolute obsession with me—and that is the returning of American poetry to the mainstream of international literature.

I have said on lectures that the source of infection in Czechoslovakia was the Viola, the nightclub. They used to read Ferlinghetti and Ginsberg to records by Thelonious Monk. They originally wanted to call the club The Cellar. But then somebody had a chick named Viola so they called it Viola. But, believe me, there never was a club between wars in Prague called the Swanee River where they could read Allen Tate to Stephen Foster. That didn't occur! Today we are all a part of the world literature, and we have a profound effect on world literature.

You get off a plane and a guy picks you up from the Society of Cultural Relations in Germany. He says, "I understand you live just a little ways from the commune of The Mothers," or, "I understand John Handy is a friend of yours . . ." Now he'd say—and don't think he wouldn't—"Have you heard Dave Meltzer's latest record?" The San Francisco scene dominates world culture.

Between the wars, an extraordinary combination of Ku Kluxers and bankrupt Trotskyites in New York dominated American literature and made it totally provincial. American literature was back where it was before the Revolutionary War. It was a provincial imitation of English baroque literature . . . Anne Bradstreet. It had no connection.

You talk to these people about contemporary literature and they don't know who you are talking about. Allen Tate, for instance, is a good friend of mine, but Allen Tate goes over to Europe and you discover that he lives entirely within the world of Paris-America . . . he doesn't know anybody . . .

they are shut away from the whole . . . you see, the world economic crisis obliterated the whole Paris-America scene. A person like Eugene Jolas and a magazine like *transition* became inconceivable . . . and this all led to the provincialization of American literature.

DM: It lasted quite a while, didn't it?

KR: Oh, Christ! Since most of the people, except the southern agrarians, had been onetime Stalinists, they just took over all the techniques of Stalinism . . . you know, hatchet reviews and logrolling and wire-pulling and controls of foundations and academic jobs and so forth . . . they had the thing absolutely by the balls, just like the Commies had had it just before them. If you got in the *Partisan Review* you could put up your little pattie and get a job on any English faculty in the USA.

We fought these people continuously . . . a lot of them had been taking exercises so that they could keep fit when they were put in the prisons during the coming war, the Imperialist War, and what happened? They were all in the OSS and now the CIA. They all were! Every single motherfucking one of them was! Name anyone that wasn't! I know all of these people. They were all chairborne on a gravy train of human blood. And don't think that we didn't say so. We said so continuously. I mean, we never stopped! Once I pinned the name "Pillowcase Head Press School of Literature" on Red Warren and Allen Tate and John Crowe Ransom, it stuck! You have no idea the domination of these people. They are afraid of me, because they have never dominated me.

You go back to New York, immediately after the war, you know, and Phil Rahv takes you out to dinner and with tears in his eyes says, "Why don't you contribute to the magazine? Why we publish Zukofsky!" But don't forget, all these people were forgotten: Zukofsky, Walter Lowenfels . . . all these people were as though they had never been. And if you mentioned them, Rahv looked embarrassed like you had just farted.

I was at this big poetry powwow that *The Groves of Academe* was written about. They were having this long discussion on the History of American Poetry, and I said, "You have left out the whole populist period!" And they said, "Who's that?" And I said, "William Vaughn Moody, Carl Sandburg, James Oppenheim, Lola Ridge, Vachel Lindsay." (Most of whom were Socialist.) With an expression of utmost contempt on his face, "Cal" Lowell said, "Well, of course, in the West, Rexroth, you haven't learned that those poor people aren't poets at all."

I don't think they were very good, but it was a question of history . . . it wasn't a question of fashion . . .

The poems in Sandburg's first two books, before he supported the First War, are really terrific. I mean, all that stuff about dynamiters and prostitutes and so on . . . it's terrific.

We finally broke it. Nobody else broke it. We broke it. And we had damn few outlets. Most of these people are not acceptable today. A few years after the war I was asked to do a survey of modern poetry and an anthology for the *New Republic* : . . and I had Olson and Creeley and Denise Levertov and Duncan and Lamantia. I wrote an article and gathered their poems and sent the material in to the *New Republic*. I didn't hear anything, but they paid me. I said: When are you going to print it? Finally I got an abusive letter saying: "Rexroth, you and your provincial poetaster friends . . . what are you trying to do? Trying to foist something off on us?" This is the way it was. But we broke it.

Bly has done wonders. When I first met Bob, he was a real young guy and we used to talk about this domination. The young people coming up need to be reconnected with the avant-garde tradition of the world. This was something that he agreed with. This is the reason for his publishing Vallejo, Trakl, Neruda and other world poets. All you have to do is go to the university and anybody with gray hair is still teaching the seventy-seven types of ambiguity in the poetry of John Donne. Its interesting that these cats are all juicers too. They will come around here in Santa Barbara and say to me, "Say, remember that party in Berkeley when Roberta pissed out the window?" They are the greatest argument for grass that you ever saw in your life! And they are still teaching this shit. I. A. Richards, T. S. Eliot, I mean, those critical methods.

On the other hand, the people that came up after the war are now also locked into the establishment. Like LeRoi Jones. What is LeRoi Jones? Is he a genuine motherfucker? He is a college professor! How does he make his living? He has never been anything else but a college professor. If he isn't working now as a college professor it is because he is a pie-card artist. He is a professional bureaucrat. Roi's a college professor. He has never in his life been anything else.

They can't understand that they are now the establishment. Ginsberg does. Of course, Allen has ten times the brains of the rest of them. He has sense. He has a sense of what happened to him and where he is. He has insight, and of course, he has connections with the younger people. He's like Dave Tough. After all, Allen is the only beatnik who is still alive. The rest of them are dead. I mean mentally . . . Allen is never uptight. He is always available. I would go nuts if I was as available as he is. Christ, I would go out of my mind! He is always available and he is always connected with people. Gary Snyder is the same way, except it is more systematized. He's the old type really.

You go around to the universities and you meet guys that are emeritus. I had dinner once at the University of Pennsylvania with a lot of cats who remembered Ezra Pound, and they were all swingers. White-haired old men . . . seventy-five years old . . . but they were real swingers and real scholars. They knew Provençal and they knew Latin or English literature or whatever . . . and these other people don't know anything. They write a doctor's thesis on T. S. Eliot and it puts them on a step of the escalator and there they stay. Eliot! Shit! They write a doctor's thesis on Elizabeth Goudge and Ruth Suckow. You have no idea!

DM: What changes do you advocate in the university? What changes do you offer as a teacher?

KR: I don't believe in universities at all! I believe the university should be totally dissolved. I think there should be more colleges than high schools. At least as many as grammar schools. They should be in the neighborhoods. In a climate like California, most of the activity should be outside. And the teachers should be beautiful people with long white whiskers and white robes sitting under oak trees and answering questions like Krishnamurti does. Leave all this superstructure and infrastructure to the engineers, the slipstick boys. Leave the buildings to them. But the humanities, I think, should be human education, dissolved into the neighborhoods and available to anybody. Everybody, young and old, should be able to come on in and sit down. This is what we were talking about. I am no advocate of Krishnamurti— he means little to me—but his way is the way to educate people.

I point out all the time: you can't teach creativity in the university system. The creative personality survives in spite of it, by living contact. Creative education, development, liberation, occurs more often in coffee shops off campus than on the campus. If you really want to do something about creative people, move the coffee shop into the curriculum.

That's like this class of mine: we come in and we kiss one another. We play a track off the new Airplane album, or something like that, and dance. The Esalen technique applies it from the outside like a mustard plaster. I had this student who goes to Esalen all the time, and I said, "You've got to realize that unless this stuff is done in context, it is unreal . . . it is like carrying a party card in the Association for the Advancement of Cunnilingus. Like, who needs it? Who needs it?" I said, "You evolve things in the activity, the doing . . ." This was a revelation to her. She said just by being confronted by that problem, she learned more than she learned from seminar after seminar at Esalen which cost all kinds of money. More than she learned in all the group-gropes she had gone to. She learned she really didn't know how to evolve this communion out of a given context, and since she didn't know, she was fundamentally a square. Because who needs to be taught to grope? The answer is most of America. I am not putting down Esalen and its poor benighted uptights.

It takes a whole year. It's only in the spring semester that you begin to get a real interaction from your students. Everyone is relaxed and they all know one another by that time.

There's a guy on the faculty who said to me, "I don't understand what principle you are using to do this. They tell me you let your students get away with murder. How do you discipline them?" And I said, "I don't. It is all self-discipline." He said, "Well, who is the authority?" I said, "There isn't any authority." He said, "Who is responsible?" I said, "We are all responsible together." "Yes, but on what principle do you keep the thing going?" And I said, "Well, I guess you'd call it agape."

Now this man is a Ph.D., fifty years old, and he

looks at me with his mouth open, muttering: "*Agape?*" What . . . What . . .?" And I say: "Comradely love. *Agape*, it's a Greek word. The class is like an underground mass." And he mutters.

Then we talk some more and I realize what this idiot thinks I mean. A Black Mass! This shows how totally isolated he is. I mean, this is a guy who has spent his life at the bottom of a disused missile silo. I mean, he doesn't know about anything! In the first place, he had so little idea about how the universe, the world, people, were put together that he could think I could get away with a Black Mass. If I wanted to. . . . He hadn't read the newspapers, he had never heard of an underground mass. He didn't know anything about changes in the Catholic Church. I told my students about the discussion and said, "We might as well be hung for wolves as dogs." A girl said, "I'll get up on a table and take off my clothes." And another one of my students said, "I'll swing the incense pot." If a guy like George Leonard knows . . . George wrote that book, *Education and Ecstasy*. Did you ever read it? It is kind of corny . . . he belongs to that world of Howard Gossage, Jerry Et-Hopkins, and Herb Caen, the Squirt Set, the junior jet set. He can't help it. But his ideas are right.

I would like to talk about music and poetry as the real pivots, the top and bottom pivots of the door into the counterculture, into the alternative society.

The stuff that isn't a part of that, in my opinion, just doesn't count. This is not a question of fashion. But I'm inclined to think that it's not going to win. Within a fairly short time, the suppression is going to be unbelievable.

See, Americans think that there are such large numbers involved in various things that nothing can happen to them, that they are protected. For years, blacks have been saying "We got ten percent of the population." But Hitler exterminated six million Jews and six million other people in a population of sixty million. And they weren't as conspicuous, they didn't have black skin. So what is it? Twenty million blacks . . . that's nothing. They can make them into Gold Dust Twins soap and sell it at a premium in Orange County supermarkets and never miss them.

I said this long before . . . I think that if this thing isn't stopped . . . anybody who stands out, like black people or anyone else, just doesn't stand a chance anymore. They will be eliminated. I think the same is true for the counterculture. They are just not enough people, really. This is why, again, poetry and music are so important. Because all these politicos, all these guys representing somebody else's foreign office, they believe in marshaling people around like troops. Confrontations . . . horrible as the People's Park episode was, let's hope some people learned their lesson. I mean, what's this one whirlygig about a can of poison gas? Shit! That was the end of it. And here these people marching . . . thousands of people . . . up and down Telegraph Avenue, like the troops of Frederick the Great. And one little heap of junk can fly over them and scatter some dust and the thing is gone, destroyed. It's all right to say that power comes out of a gun, but, shit, man, their power comes out of the hydrogen bomb, and when push comes to shove, they have Teller's Doomsday Machine in Livermore . . . and it's good-bye. To everything!

The techniques of massive paramilitary confrontations are, in my opinion, absurd. The Sunflower Sutra has more effect than a Columbia University takeover. It does. It's just a fact. Because all you have to do is co-opt most of these people. They found it out with the blacks. All you have to do is to pick a government office at random . . . take the Yellow Pages and look up the United States government and shut your eyes and put your finger down, read the address, and go to the office. Walk into the guy and say: "You motherfucker, I am going to cut your gizzard out," and he says, "Here is a twenty-thousand-a-year job!" It's a fact!

The head of the Poverty Program in the Fillmore was a notorius three-time loser, an extortionist, somebody that no Negro would touch with a ten-foot pole with a six-inch extension. He'd been thrown out of the Muslims, been thrown out of the Panthers, been thrown out of everything . . . and here he was, the boss man. All you have to do is co-opt people like that. And if you can't co-opt them, then you destroy them.

Whereas the counterculture as a culture, as a way of life . . . you can't catch up with it, it's in the blood-stream of society. You can't pin it down. Its effect is continuously corrosive. It's these capsules they stick in people that keep feeding medicine into their blood-stream for twenty years. The more the poetry of music is massive confrontation, the less effective it is. It may be effective in a very limited range, but the other thing is effective over a long term. This is true of the whole protest-rock and protest-folk bit. Young people are wise to the fact that Donovan is more revolutionary than Dylan. The whole thing that has grown up around Leonard Cohen is more subversive than Country Joe and the Fish. And as the years go by, it becomes completely phony. Play Pete Seeger singing "I Dreamed I Saw Joe Hill Last Night" . . . it would make you throw up. . . .

DM: To my mind, Pete Seeger has always been a singer of the radical movement . . .

KR: Seeger was brought out in Café Society Downtown. Christ, that goes back a long time! It's cooked, you know. A lot of Pete's stuff is cooked. Woody was much better because he was less a part of the apparatus and more uncontrollable, more of a natural.

You used to hear cats singing in the International Labor Defense Organization, you know, records can

still be found, "Swing Low Sweet ILD," supposed to
be a Kentucky miners' song. Horseshit! That's artificial . . . that's the cooked thing! Seeger just can't
get away from it, except in some individual songs.

And people like Joan Baez, people like that, are too
innocent and they don't believe in being hypercritical.
I don't know a single song of Joan's, either on record
or in concert, that is that kind of cooked party-line
stuff—whether it is anarchist or Communist. She
doesn't do things like that. That's her instinctive taste.
If you were to talk to Joan about things like this, she
would be offended. She thinks I am a baddie. She
doesn't like me at all because I am a man of violence.

Look at the effect she has had. Her effect is radi-
cally subversive. There's a wonderful story about
Joan Baez. She was responsible for the big Wolf
Bierman bust in East Berlin. They had a Vietnam
thing in East Berlin and Joan gets up after Bierman
has sung and says, "I am going to sing a song dedicated to my good comrade Wolf Bierman. The song is
called 'Freiheit.' " Joan sings the song in German. The
next day they called Bierman down and said, "What
does she mean 'comrade'?" He said, "She isn't my
responsibility, I didn't have anything to do with
it. . . ." They told him to give in his work permit and
his travel permit . . . they busted him for a year.

Joan gets very few dates in the hard Iron Curtain
countries like Bulgaria, East Germany, and Russia.
She has been to Czechoslovakia, Yugoslavia, and I
guess Romania. She may have gone to Poland during
the thaw. But they all know. When she gets up and
sings "Barbara Allen" it is subversive.

The real thing about your stuff, or Joni Mitchell's
stuff, for all kinds of people like this, and all kinds of
people that are not getting recorded and booked, is
that it involves and presents a pattern of human
relationships which is unassimilable by the society.
What the songs speak of cannot be assimilated. I

mean, here is a love song . . . but the kind of love it sings of can't exist in this society. The song gets out like a bit of radioactive cobalt. It just foments subversion around itself as long as it is available. I think this is much more important. Because everything else can be crushed.

I mean, you can have wonderful communes in New Mexico, or sleep under a tree, or sleep in a canyon, but you never heard of a latrine there, and the food is always burned, and the kids get ringworm . . . in New Mexico they play with the Spanish kids and get lice and pretty soon the thing falls apart because they don't know how to live and all the Gary Snyders in the world aren't going to teach them. I mean he can't go on handing out merit badges in Woods Communes forever. It ain't going to do them a fucking bit of good. He is going to get tired of saying, "A real Zen master says, 'Don't shit on the ground, especially alongside the sleeping bag.'" It's not going to have any effect. These people are all vulnerable and they are still living on money from papa and mama. And they are all rich. When those people hit New Mexico, it was amazing how those people went and bought up land. And they are still buying it up. And the land has tripled in price!

DM: It seems clear that so much of the revolution is middle-class consumer oriented. The middle class consumes revolution, makes it into stuff, goods, and takes the life out of it.

KR: Yes, of course . . . that's why the spades hate it. You know, Hannibal Williams? He's a guy that has been fighting Relocation in the Western Addition's Citizens' Organization. Hannibal is a very nice guy and I remember having a discussion in the coffee shop in the Howard Church. I had just come back from Europe and the flower children had decayed, and it was obvious that the Mafia had taken over the neighborhood. This conference was all about the relation of the hippie community to the Haight-Ashbury resident community, primarily black. And, of course, the reason the Haight-Ashbury developed was that it was red San Francisco. It was full of retired longshore organizers whose kids now smoke pot and sing Pete Seeger . . . and blacks . . . it's a genuinely integrated neighborhood. That's how the people got in. They wouldn't have gotten to first base if they had gone to the Sunset or Richmond District.

Anyway, some guy got up and said he had just hitchhiked from a very rich suburb, and he was stoned, and dirty, and he was fat and had a lot of beads, and the hippie stuff he wore was all new . . . and he said something about the relation between the hip community and the straight community. I was going to say something but Hannibal jumped up and said, "You got it right, man, but you got it ass backwards! You are the straight community and the community you are invading is the hip community! You come into this neighborhood and you imitate my clothes. I wear blue jeans because I go to work! You even smear paint and plaster on them . . . yet you wouldn't know which end of a paint brush to hold! And you take over my house or my flat and you play my music on your fucking two-thousand-dollar hi-fi sets, which you turn up so loud you keep my children awake all night!"

When he got through, the people reeled . . . but then it reeled right off of them. . . .

Allen Cohen, who was editing and putting out the *Oracle* at that time, attacked me. And I said, "Look here, it's true! You are all engaged in a bourgeois enterprise. Don't shit me, man! You are a business-man! You are engaged in a bourgeois enterprise! Face the fact that you are middle-class . . ."

On the Great Grass Road, you know, you find a chick dead in a ditch fifty miles out of Kabul, bare-foot, clothed only in a blanket with a hole in the middle of it and a rope around her waist, and she's got a bindle, a bag, and in it is a diary about all the Arab truck drivers she's sucked off, and been cornholed by, and strapped to one leg she has two hypodermics and some medicine . . . and strapped to the other leg, ten-thousand-dollars in travelers checks! That's an actual case. There are thousands of them . . . all you have to do is just make the Great Grass Road . . . go from one of those places to another, from Casablanca on . . . you can't pass Burma . . . to Calcutta. These people are all rich. I mean, rich, not just middle class!

The real far-out hippie is the person who is actually engaged in a personal revolt against the very evil family, a corrupt society and so forth. It is not a massive social phenomenon, except it is a social phenomenon reflecting the collapse of this society. People are crazy enough to think it's the revolution. I mean, this is ridiculous. It is as ridiculous as believing that the circle of princesses around Rasputin was the revolution. Because it is the same thing. Exactly the same thing. There's not the slightest bit of difference between Rasputin's circle and upper-middle-class hippie life.

DM: A majority of the new consumers consider themselves to be the revolution because they are consuming the cultural ideas of what is relevant: the records, the books, stuff like that . . .

KR: You see, you have to draw a line. A lot of these people just don't know anything at all. All they are interested in is cunt or cock and dope . . . and preferably spade meat. . . .

Down the street from me in San Francisco is a so-called shoeshine parlor. I don't know why they don't call it an athletic club. The only thing they use the shoeshine stand for . . . I pass by sometimes and the door is open and some chick is balling some guy . . . these old cats in bib overalls: asphalt spreaders and

ditch diggers and one thing and another . . . middle-
aged blacks, most of them juiced all the time. These
chicks . . . will fly to San Francisco from Sweet Briar
and they take a cab from the airport to the Haight-
Ashbury. They go to a Salvation Army and get some
old rags and real hip threads and they buy some beads
at the Psychedelic Shop, and they head down Haight
Street. And they come to the shoeshine parlor and
there will be a big old black grandpa leaning up
against the window, chewing snuff and juiced out of
his mind and dirt all over his bib overalls and a
chick will walk up to him and say, "Sir, would you
care to enjoy my body?" This scares the shit out of
these guys when it first happens! And they will come
to me and say, "Mr. Ken, what is this? Are these
chicks crazy?" And the young chicks go back to
Sweet Briar and they say: "Girls, do you want to
come up to my room? I had a lover in San Francisco
. . . an authentic Negro. And I have the most interesting little parasites. They are the same kind that
Negroes have. They are called crabs and I want to
show them to you!"

Like the cat Hannibal had the rap with—I said to
him, "When do you think *Howl* was written?" He
said, "Huh man?" I said, "You know, *Howl*, Ginsberg
. . . the Ginsberg that runs the secondhand clothing
store at Fillmore and Haight . . ." (there isn't any
such place). He said, "Oh, yeah, man, I get all my
threads there. . . ." I told Hannibal that I didn't invent this guy, God sent him to me.

The reading that we gave for the Planning and
Conservation League (June 30, 1969, Norse Auditorium) was very significant. Because in the first
place, nobody really knew who they were. I'm supposed to know all this stuff and I didn't know anything about it. But everybody responded immediately
to what it was and the people came out. And the
people who came out were very interesting. The last

benefit that I had read at was for the Free Medical Clinic at the Straight Theater. There was all the difference in the world. Because that Norse Auditorium conservation thing was full of flower children. It was full of people like the people were five years ago. They were serious people . . . they weren't meth heads . . . they were an entirely different kind of people than those who would be brought out for something in the heart of Haight Street. They knew, they were well informed. They knew who the poets were at the reading, and they had also come out for this ecological bit. We forget that this thing is going on under all the noise.

On the other hand, there is this thing which is strictly controlled by the Mafia. The world of the zombies in the Haight-Ashbury. They are not interested in all that psychedelic boloney, that everybody was talking about before. They don't want that. They want massive destruction right away. They don't want any LSD . . . they are not interested in that . . . or an expanding consciousness . . . they want to get stoned. They want to stay stoned. Like hit on the head with a half-ton stone.

You remember the cat they arrested? They took him to the Park Station because he had been going around the neighborhood, up and down the street, telling people that he had a peace pill to sell. He said that he had a friend that worked in the chemical warfare laboratory and that he stole this stuff and pressed it into pills . . . and he told his customers that it was a fifty-fifty chance that the pill would either give you the greatest high you ever had, stone you out of your mind for four days, or it would kill you. A fifty-fifty chance. And all it would cost would be ten dollars. The cops busted him and they were going to beat the shit out of him . . . but he said, "Look, man, it is just an aspirin." So the cops let him go. But it shows . . . he was making all kinds of money selling aspirin tablets that might kill you. It is so easy to confuse the two things.

These rabid apologists for the dope culture, like Burroughs, they confuse the issue. Of course, Allen to a certain extent did that for a while. All this stuff of Alan Watts' . . . I think the two things are quite different, and I think you lose sight of the lost dogs that are running around, of what is really going on underneath. These people may dress the same, but actually with a sharp eye you can distinguish the differences.

Here is a chick in a poncho and tights and beads made out of chicken vertebrae around her neck. And here is another chick and she seems to be dressed just the same, but you can tell the difference . . . it's a subtle thing. Yet neither one of them comes from the working class . . . they are upper middle class. They are people who are opting out of the military-indus-trial society. They wouldn't have the option if they weren't up at the top of it. You can't get any options otherwise.

5

KR: For those people that we fought as they grew up, poetry is an important experience. Poetry is life affirmation, they really dig all this Gary Snyder bear-shit-on-the-trail poetry, they have contact with nature, and, of course, as you know, the genuine ecological revolution's rolling now and involving thousands.

If Diane Di Prima had stayed making the scene around Tompkins Square she would never be writing for an ecological crisis newssheet. And don't forget KPFA's connection with all of this. KPFA has given hundreds of programs, thousands of programs, in the past twenty years on the ecological crisis. And I, on my own program, have never let up on it. There has never been a book, even a bad book, on ecology and on the environmental problem that I haven't reviewed and used the book as a peg to hang a long ecology speech on. KPFA has had countless people of importance talking about Famine II, and Famine III and Famine IV. And all this DDT uproar that has now hit the paper. The DDT thing has been about on KPFA for over ten years, since the first evidence began to come in.

The use of the power structure, the subversive use of their techniques by Dave Brower was decried immediately by his old rock climbing comrades—who are now corporation lawyers and other shits of that sort. I mean, fuck, these people who are corporation lawyers, they know perfectly well that the success of a business is measured by its indebtedness! I mean, that's the way you measure a business. A successful business owes five million bucks, and an unsuccessful one owes nothing. They accused Dave Brower of running up enormous debts for the Sierra Club. Yet he was using the techniques, the basic techniques: utilizing the bourgeois publishing scene, Madison Avenue, lobbies, everything his detractors' clients used all the time. This is what happened in the Sierra Club. They objected to Dave Brower because he was fundamentally subversive. They made the most shameful appeals! "How we used to have a good ole hiking club and used to go out and eat peanut butter soup and put raspberry jam on the snow in the passes . . ." and all this kind of crap. Well, the "good old days" are gone. Very few people in Berkeley know this, but there is a native son and daughter Berkeley establishment that really runs the university. They are also the people that run the Sierra Club, and, of course, they think they are the most liberal souls on earth. But the ecological crisis is of such a grievous nature that it is only by the most massive action that anything will happen at all . . . and probably what should happen is not going to happen. You know, there is no way of extrapolating into the future that will be effective. The only people who know this as a mass, all of a sudden, are the counterculture who latched onto it because it explains what is happening.

All this struggle against papas and mammas, in which idiots lead mass demonstrations in Berkeley and think they have the offensive, they don't have the offensive at all, they have the defensive. I mean, it is the papas and mammas that have the offensive. This is why it has such a family character, because it is a fundamentally . . . it is a phenomenon of species death due to the breakdown of the biota of the ecological relationship.

A few years ago they were saying the reason the dinosaurs became extinct was because the vulcanism of the Jurassic filled the sky with dust, and cooled the climate and the marshes got too cold for the dinosaurs' balls, and so they became infertile. Well, the dinosaurs didn't become extinct because they had cold balls. They ate all their eggs. Say this and people who are listening dig it. It's like being converted to Methodism. The whole thing clears up. They can understand what it is all about. And this is why the whole ecological thing that Gary's been preaching— you know, he has made himself the leader of it—is so important. It is the key.

Charismatic, you see, everybody says bolshevism

broke down, that other things were never tried because they could not envisage a real alternative that would work or, to use correctly the misused slang, a "viable alternative," something that wouldn't be stillborn. An ecological revolution can scientifically extrapolate into the future certain essential conditions. It can say this and this must occur. There must be so many people to so many acres. There must be so many people to so many square feet. There must be certain kinds of relationships, certain kinds of agriculture: there are all kinds of things that must be and this necessitates certain methods of production and distribution, etc. You create, as they say in science or math, a model and it is a clear model. The Bolsheviks had no model. They had no model at all.

It is just like the blacks. They have stopped doing this, but whites used to say: "What do you Negroes want?" And people like Roi would say, "That's your problem, motherfucker." Well, they don't say it anymore, because you can't do anything with that. After a while you get your head beat in, you get shot. "That's your problem, motherfucker" is not a sufficient prescription for the future. You don't want to go out and get yourself killed for that.

The ecologic crisis provides—the way that Marxism with all its bullshit about scientific socialism never did—a scientific model for a just society. The interesting thing is that this resembles far more the thing that Marx and Engels attacked: utopian socialism.

You want to know what the future should be like? It should be like William Morris's *News from Nowhere*. He was more right than Marx. He talks about an idyllic underpopulated England with the old type of Japanese gardening and pre-Raphaelite costumes. And he is right and Marx is wrong. Until recently Doxiadis was talking about a world of two hundred billion people, all kinds of shit like that, and then suddenly he woke up. I used to argue this with him. Then I met him in Athens recently and he had awakened. He has become obsessed now because it had come to face him: the famous honey of Hymettus, the long mountain above Athens, is no longer available. The bees are gone. They have gone over to the other side of the mountain. Athens is like San Francisco. It is a wind-swept city, but the smog has driven the bees off the slopes of Hymettus . . . so Doxiadis doesn't talk about two hundred billion people living on the earth anymore.

Look inside the iron curtain countries. Part of the revolt against Moscow has been that formerly orthodox Marxists have said, "Look, man, we are up to our asses in steel mills. We need uniformly planned development for a stable population, and we don't want to be a breadbasket for Moscow." The thing that has really turned me against communism, I mean, orthodox Bolshevism, long long ago, was not the Moscow trials or the expulsion of Trotsky or the right wing, or the trials of the engineers, or anything like that at all. I expected most of that, even as a kid. It was this.

The Russians used to put out a magazine called the *Economic Review of the Soviet Union*. I had a job for the *Nation*, or some fellow-traveler periodical, I was asked to write an article on the Soviet lumber industry. So I did. Out of the *Economic Review of the Soviet Union*, which had various references, I got information and did a tremendous lot of research. They brief all this stuff in English. They put out scholarly publications in agriculture in the days before Stalin killed them. They would have briefs in the back of the trade papers in French or English. Knowing a little about lumbering, I discovered that the Russians were doing the most ruthless and destructive lumbering in the world. And, furthermore, it was being done by slave labor. That Weyerhaeuser was the Sierra Club in comparison to what they were doing in the mountains of Georgia, or the forests at the edge of the tundra. I became more interested and I discovered that there wasn't any difference. It is all, East and West, production for production's sake. No human values are involved.

The Chinese know this, but the Chinese can't deal with the problem because they have an enormous reforestation difficulty. They plant twenty trees here, yet they have to cut down two hundred there because of population pressure. The two different agencies in the country work at cross-purposes.

You see, this involves an important matter: human relationships. Human relationships that are expressed in the lyrics of the best modern songs. Human relationships in song that is unassimilable. These are ecologically sound relationships. They imply a society which is quite different and the difference is an ecological difference. Everything ties into it.

Right now there is a Moholy-Nagy show here. I knew Moholy . . .

We went with a student of mine, a girl, and she thought it was great. She was very excited, but my ex-wife, Marie, and Carol, and I—we were very depressed. In each one of those little pictures and circles and squares and lines, Moholy thought he had something that would reform the world . . . it would go out from the painting and create a new society. He thought that it would do this by using the production methods of capitalism. He was wrong and failed. He was absorbed as a design consultant. There are Moholy-Nagys all over typography ever since. The whole Bauhaus scene . . . that's what it all meant. And of course, that doesn't mean much to people anymore, now. Who takes Bauhaus-art-style classes in modern art anymore? The professors don't explain this to anybody, and they don't understand that this is what it was all about. It is all so tragic to see those beautiful pictures and to think they are all essentially failures because they didn't do what they were intended to do.

The whole problem is to find works of art which remain permanently unassimilable and permanently corruptive. This means that they don't really differ very much from anybody else's work of art. The songs of Shakespeare are permanently indigestible and permanently subversive.

I think we have talked long enough.

Summer, 1969

William Everson
(Brother Antoninus)

1

WE: Leaving the Order was more of an upheaval than a decision. That's one reason I'm still at sea. I just plunged out. I should have waited for the expiration of my temporary vows next October when I would either make final profession or leave legitimately.

The reasons I didn't are really personal ones and would take too long to lay bare. I've been too close to them to analyze them. I . . . Susanna . . . when the father of her child, you know, that off-again, on-again thing . . . when that wouldn't resolve, when they really couldn't find their way to make a life together, it kept throwing me back into the picture as a—as a what? Not an alternative, certainly. I was in her life before him. I think, really, that her bid for a marriage with him was an attempt to find an alternative to me. And when it didn't work out—even with the arrival of their baby, no marriage was forthcoming—I began to sense that my number was up. So I went to Europe last summer, really an attempt to get away, to change the focus so as to allow every opportunity for the other thing to prevail. Then I came back and it hadn't and it didn't and it wasn't. In November I went on my regular eastern tour. By the end of that month I realized that what I was returning to was something permanent, that I could no longer delude myself that this was a transitional involvement. That did it. I moved then to make the break with the Order. At my final reading at Davis in December I closed by pulling off my habit and leaving the stage. The price I must pay, of course, is that I am out of the sacraments.

JS: That must have played some part in influencing your decision. You knew before, didn't you, that you would be out of the sacraments? Will you attempt to get some dispensation?

WE: Yes. It seems we may be able to marry in the Church. At least, that's my hope.

DM: You really haven't left the faith as much as the Order?

WE: That's right. I'm still a Catholic.

JS: Why don't you bring us up to date by telling us a bit about your life prior to your initial conversion experiences? When you were William Everson, the printer. I guess that's what I heard about you first.

WE: Well, actually, printing came late with me, although I was born in a printshop, so to speak. Being the son of a printer I experienced the atmospherics of it very early. But what with the powerful presence of the father, and being in one of the basic Oedipal situations . . . man, I got out of there fast! So it wasn't until after I became a poet that I began to recognize my lost opportunities. But the printing really didn't develop until Waldport. We needed a press badly up there and when we got one I began to print in earnest.

DM: Waldport . . . the CO camp?

WE: Yes.

JS: Did you go there out of high school?

WE: No, no. I was thirty years old. High school was the Depression. I graduated in 1931, down in the San Joaquin Valley. Then I tried a semester at Fresno State and dropped out and went back home. My only work was summer work at the Libby McNeil cannery, as a syrup maker, with idleness in the winters, pretty much trying to find myself. In 1933 I entered the CCC and a year later left that to go back to Fresno State. This time I encountered the work of Robinson Jeffers and at last came to terms with myself as a poet.

DM: Were you writing then?

WE: I only began to write in earnest after I found Jeffers. Before that, it could have been music or art or literature. I was trying all three. But when I encountered Jeffers suddenly everything coalesced. I found my voice, began to speak in my own right. I left college to go back to the land, to get married and plant a vineyard. I put my roots down and was making a life of it. But the war pulled me out-of that. And it was the war that really forced me to shape up. I don't know how else to put it. Being uprooted was a crushing blow, but it proved to be the breakover point I needed. In retrospect I can see that I had to get out of the Valley. But I couldn't see it then.

JS: And you were arrested and tried?

WE: No. my claim for conscientious objector status was accepted. I went right into the camp as part of the regular CPS quota. Civilian Public Service, that was the euphemism.

JS: So you were called to alternative service?

WE: They sent me there. I didn't choose it. They sent me there.

DM: I guess, that really was the only legitimate alternate to military service?

WE: No, there was what was called Detached Service, work in hospitals and on dairy farms. I didn't opt for that. Actually, there were three alternatives. One was 1AO in the military service, noncombatant. This is the one the government wanted us to do, made every effort to get COs to accept.

DM: You mean medic . . .?

WE: Yes. Then there was Detached Service, work at specified mental hospitals and dairy farms. And finally there were the camps, work with the Forest Service.

JS: And that was what Waldport was?

WE: Yes.

DM: You were kept there in a restricted kind of environment?

WE: There weren't any guards or barbed wire, but if you left, the FBI was after you. When you were caught you went to prison. Mussolini did the same thing with political dissidents before the war—sent them to work camps in the mountains and, if they left, clapped them in prisons. The comparison is only approximate because ours was a true alternative to combat duty. But the injustice lay in the fact that there was no pay. Under the Emancipation Proclamation, involuntary servitude is outlawed. No citizen can be made to work without pay except as punishment for a crime. The draft did call for equal pay with the armed forces but Roosevelt feared a pacifist resistance movement and saw to it that Congress never appropriated the money. And it never has.

DM: Weren't there several other artists and writers there?

WE: Actually a good deal of what later happened in the San Francisco scene had its origin right there in Waldport. The Interplayers began there. Adrian Wilson, one of our ablest printers, got his start there. James Harmon, who later edited *The Ark*, was there.

I never think of Harmon without recalling an episode that is still, as they say, etched on my memory:

the encounter with Dreiser. It was on my first furlough, the furlough of 1943. Harmon and I got leave to go down to San Francisco. We took the coast stage south to Marshfield where we had to lay over in order to pick up the Portland bus southbound for San Francisco the next morning.

As we boarded the bus in Marshfield I noticed a man who seemed familiar. I said to myself, "That man looks like Theodore Dreiser." Harmon said it couldn't be, but Jeffers had spoken of Dreiser as a "tough old mastodon," and that's just the way this character looked. Hulking shoulders. Slack jaws. Strangely inattentive eyes that missed nothing. Even in his photographs his configuration was unmistakable.

During the war the bus travel was simply awful. In order to save rubber the law held their schedule down to thirty-five miles an hour, but the drivers went like hell between stops and waited at the next depot for time to catch up. So we had plenty of opportunity to look each other over.

At Gold Beach, Oregon, we pulled in for lunch. By this time I was sure it was Dreiser. As Harmon and I got ready to sit down Harmon forgot about lunch and followed the man into the lavatory. He came right out as if he'd really found gold on that beach. "It's him!" he exclaimed excitedly. "Its Dreiser, all right. Come on!"

Even as I got up I had my misgivings but curiosity got the better of judgment. Dreiser was standing at the urinal relieving himself, and not knowing what else to do I began to talk. I had never read any of his books, so I began with us. It was a fatal mistake.

"Mr. Dreiser," I began, "we're two poets on furlough from a camp in Waldport. We are going down to San Francisco. We hope to meet some of the other writers there and renew our acquaintance with the literary scene . . ."

Dreiser looked at me and I suddenly discovered I had nothing more to say. He slowly buttoned his fly, and as he turned to wash his hands, he said two words with extreme irony: "So what!"

Then he started in. Ripping a paper towel from the rack, he crumbled it in those fearsome hands and proceeded with contempt. "There are thousands of you. You crawl about the country from conference to literary conference. You claim to be writers, but what do you ever produce? Not one of you will amount to a goddamn. You have only the itch to write, nothing more . . . the insatiable itch to express yourself. Everwhere I go I run into you, and I'm sick of you. The world is being torn apart in agony, crying out for truth, the terrible truth. And you . . ." He paused and his voice seemed to suddenly grow weary. "You have nothing to say."

I turned to go. Harmon was already gone. Opening the door into the restaurant, I looked back to let him know how sorry I was that I had accosted him, but I couldn't open my mouth. Then Dreiser stepped past me, as if I had opened the door only for him. For a moment the contempt seemed to fade from his face and a kind of geniality gleamed there. "Well," he said, "take it easy. It lasts longer that way." Then he was gone.

Not really gone. His seat was ahead of ours, and we had already noticed that he was traveling with a young woman. After Gold Beach, aware of our presence behind him, he kept stiffly aloof, conversing with her circumspectly. But far down the coast, at the end of the long hot afternoon, when everyone was collapsed with fatigue, she could stand it no longer. Reaching out her hand she stroked with tender fondness the balding head. Dazed with exhaustion he accepted it gratefully until he remembered us. Suddenly thrashing his head like a mastodon caught red-handed in a pterodactyl's nest he flung the hand from him. She never tried that again.

DM: Fantastic. . . . But getting back to Waldport, how did so many artists happen to arrive there?

WE: The setup was like this. In 1940 when France fell, the draft was instituted here although the country had no expectation of going to war. The law allowed for conscientious objection based on religious conviction, categorically defined as membership in one of the "three historic peace churches." Actually, individual draft boards applied it more broadly.

In order to avoid the merciless treatment of COs in World War I (and Cummings' poem *I Sing of Olaf* gives us a glimpse of that) the peace churches stepped in and proposed an alternative along the lines of the CCC, which was still in operation, and which provided a good model to follow. In the CCC operation the army reserves ran the camp program and the Forest Service ran the work program. What the peace churches proposed was that if they could run the camp program in place of the army reserves they would pay for maintenance out of their own pocket. And this is what the government accepted. But it meant we had to go into a religiously oriented camp and many of us didn't like that because we were not orthodox Christians.

So we arrived at these camps under the authority of some church group—either the Quakers or the Mennonites or the so called Brethren, historically the Dunkers. The Quakers were the most favored by nonconformists because they were the most liberal. The Mennonites were the most disliked because they were the most conservative. The Brethren camps were ranked somewhere in between, and that's what I found myself in at Waldport.

The churches early began setting up special schools in certain camps so that men interested in a given project could transfer there and participate in that activity. The government didn't object so long as the work program wasn't affected. Before Waldport, the special schools were for such studies as Cooperative Management, Pacifist Philosophy, etc. At Waldport we proposed an Arts project and were accepted. On the basis of this we began to attract artists from camps all over the country. That is, until the Forest Service Director put the kibosh on it when he saw that most of them were goldbrickers as far as his work project was concerned. But by that time, we had our nucleus.

DM: You established a press there?

WE: Yes, the Untide Press. Actually, before it was over three publications were coming out of Waldport. The *Illiterati* came to us from Cascade Locks in Oregon and *Compass* magazine came to us from Maryland. Each kept its editorial distinctness.

DM: Did you do a lot of printing for the Untide Press?

WE: Yes. Our big problem was of course the presswork. Eventually we received by transfer a real printer, a pressman, from Michigan. He had no love for the Arts program (an incredible suspicion and hostility to these special schools prevailed among the camps generally, a real anti-intellectualist bias) but Kalal helped us. I pumped him for everything he knew about presswork, and he knew plenty.

JS: Did they allow you to do this instead of presswork?

WE: No, this was work done after hours.

JS: You would work a full day and then go and do presswork?

WE: That's right. Nine hours of project work each day and then to the press to work in the evenings.

DM: *These Are the Ravens* is your first book. Was it published at the camp?

WE: Much earlier. It was printed over in San Leandro in 1935. There was a vanity publisher there, Hans A. Hoffman, who had a little mag called *Westward*. He printed conventional middle-class poetry. Ladies with three names, that sort of thing. But he accepted some of my open-form poems and I was jubilant, my first magazine publication off campus. When he announced a pamphlet series, I wrote to him about it. The uniform format called for an edition of one thousand copies to sell for ten cents each. The author paid thirty dollars for the job. The publisher kept half the edition to sell, paying the author one-half cent per copy sold. The author kept the other five hundred copies to sell for himself. Thirty dollars was a lot of money in 1935, but I was making syrup at a cannery in Sunnyvale that summer and I swung it.

DM: How long were you interned at Waldport?

WE: Three-and-one-half years.

DM: When you left Waldport, where did you go?

WE: Right back here to San Francisco because of Rexroth. You see, when the war was over and they began to demobilize, they could have closed the entire system of CO camps right off. But because of their notions of equity and the political instinct to prevent the complaints of returning GIs that we got first crack at the jobs, the government made us wait until they could demobilize those thirteen million fighting men. We found ourselves waiting interminably. VJ day was in August of 1945 and I was not released until late in July 1946, and I wasn't the last by any means. And the only reason we were kept that long was so that we would not be released ahead of the men who were inducted at the same time as we were.

DM: When did you first come in contact with Rexroth?

WE: Let's say about 1944. I got a letter from him when I was in camp. Somebody had sent him one of my CO pamphlets, *The Waldport Poems* or *War Elegies*, I don't remember which. On my next furlough (we got furloughs on the same basis as the soldiers) I came down to San Francisco to meet him, and his presence here was the real reason I returned after the war. Not only was he the acknowledged leader of the new literary ferment, but as soon as I read his new poems, *The Phoenix and the Tortoise,* I took him to be the best poet of his generation. I've never really doubted that. It was a tough generation to be born into, because following the brilliant coterie of writers born in the nineties—the Hart Crane generation—those born in the first decade of this century couldn't sustain that kind of esprit de corps, and the baton went to England: the Auden-Spender generation. But of the Americans, Rexroth remains the best. Better than Eberhardt, who has won all the awards. Better than Kunitz, the supertechnician. Better even than Roethke, who is of course the ranking poet of that generation.

Both Roethke and Rexroth were born in the Midwest, but whereas Rexroth came West, Roethke went East. It was fatal for him. He could have been—ought to have been—the Theodore Dreiser of American poetry, but he opted instead for prestige and technical proficiency. The prestige he got but the proficiency remained very limited, actually. He constantly celebrated rapture but could never let go. He mastered certain forms and these are impressive, but his open-form experiments of the later years were not. In contradistinction, the open form of Rexroth is brilliant and vivid, his sense of the earth is immediate and pungent. Gary Snyder, for instance, the best earth-man now writing, stands squarely on Rexroth's shoulders. Rexroth is more uneven than Roethke, granted, but that's because he risks more, attempts more. Though in the modernist tradition actually his classical sense is far more haunting and evocative than Roethke's doctrinaire aesthetic classicism. His masterpiece is the title poem of *The Phoenix and the Tortoise,* in my view the best poem of World War II. Unless Lowell's *Quaker Graveyard* is really that. I've long wanted to do a piece on Kenneth, but his erudition is overwhelming. I'm not capable of coming to terms with it. Anyway, it was his presence here in San Francisco that drew me when the camps finally closed.

Of course, there was the fact that my wife was here. But we were so estranged by that time, it was hopeless. Sometimes she came up to Waldport but we were never able to straighten it out. She fell in love with a young friend of mine even before she left the Valley for San Francisco. That affair went on all through my time in camp and it was this that I couldn't abide. *Chronicle of Division* in *The Residual Years* spells it out. So by war's end there really wasn't much hope of salvaging the marriage. When I look back on it I think we could have resumed our life together, but I was sensitive and proud, and very very hurt. I'm certain now that she was ready to take up the relationship again but I was just too proud, just too hurt.

JS: Did you go back to cannery work?

WE: No, I came down here and joined a group on a farm outside of Sebastopol. We were going to make a life on the land together—the commune idea that's so fetching now with the hippies. Rexroth was going to join us. I actually moved my handpress there and installed it in an old apple dryer, but I met Mary Fabilli, and as soon as I met her I fell in love with her. I left the farm and followed her back to Berkeley. The poems in the third section of *The Residual Years* are all the product of this change. In Berkeley I got a job as the janitor at the University of California and then moved the press back and began to print my poems.

DM: Were you a Catholic at that time?

WE: Lord, no. I was anti-Catholic. It was Mary who converted me. She was fallen away herself but had already begun the painful process of struggling back. You might say I was her last fling!

DM: Did she actively try to convert you?

WE: God, yes! Mary dominated the relationship to the end. She's a powerful personality, and I was confused, lost within myself and really looking for anchorage. It was her strong hand, no doubt about it, that drew me into the Church.

On the other hand, in my own defense, I'm not saying that a masterful woman simply got me by the nose and pulled me into this monolithic religion. I was really looking for what the Church is, though I didn't know it. I didn't know I needed the sacramental life. She brought me that, and I've never regretted it.

DM: The ritual, the structure . . .

WE: Yes. If you are a religious man without a religion you're in trouble. Mary gave me that religion, the vocabulary, the conceptual background. And also the faith, the belief. It was really the great turning point in my life.

DM: Do you think that initially it was a philosophical conversion and later an emotional one?

WE: No. The other way around. It's possible that I sensed a whole new field of engagement remaining untried even as I met her. Certainly my pantheism had reached its term. In the breakup of my first marriage I would cry out to God and there just wasn't any answer coming back. Pantheism is really a great concept, but there's not much help from it when your life needs help most. It just isn't personal enough to meet the absolute demand of the spirit.

JS: In conversion, you generally think of the mind leading, or the heart . . .

WE: Well, this was a conversion of the heart, but

with the mind running like crazy to catch up. I went into the Order to enable the mind to catch up with where the heart was.

DM: Then you and Mary split?

WE: Not just to enter the Order, I would never have done that. But before I could be baptized we had to separate because of the validity of my first marriage. And of course her first marriage was valid too. She married Grif Borjesen in the Church even though she was no longer a committed Catholic. In order to satisfy her parents. Which is foolish. But that's the way born Catholics do.

JS: So you couldn't get special permission to . . .?

WE: The norms then were so tight, so legalistic. To get an annulment you had to produce legal evidence of coercion or of nonbelief. Apparently the Church is more willing to take your word for it now.

JS: You were both struggling Catholics and yet they wouldn't allow you the sacrament?

WE: Not as long as we stayed together. We tried to get permission to live "as brother and sister" as it's called, cohabitation without sexual intercourse. But they said we were too young. And we were. They were right! [*Laughter.*]

DM: After all this trouble, what did you and Mary decide?

WE: It wasn't a matter of having to agree to enter an order or anything like that. We just had to separate to receive the sacraments. Once we were not living together she was free to reenter the sacraments and I was free to get baptized, which I did. I stayed on in Mary's house because my press was there. She was most generous about that, renting another room for herself and letting me stay on alone there. And as luck or grace would have it my Guggenheim came through at that moment. Boy, that was a beautiful year, in spite of the pain of another separation. I worked that Guggenheim year! I was printing and binding and writing like crazy, just like crazy! 1949. Twenty years ago! Oh, man!

So I didn't travel on my Guggenheim, which actually I should have done, from the point of view of tactics. New Directions had published *The Residual Years* the year before, and if I'd used my Guggenheim to go East and stump the campuses, that book would have sold. But I hung right in there and wrote. I wrote so much some of it is still unpublished.

I bound *The Privacy of Speech* that summer, and in the fall was getting ready to print *In The Fictive Wish,* but my need for a more structured religious life was beginning to assert itself, and instead I began to search for an order.

I couldn't find one to meet my needs. The Dominicans were there but I never approached them. They didn't seem reclusive enough for me. I talked to the Benedictines and the Franciscans. I didn't go to the Trappists because Merton was there, and his *Seven Storey Mountain* had made that route a bit too faddish at that time. Besides, their entrance requirements were strict, and with the impediment of a marriage in my background I stood little chance of acceptance. So I talked to the Benedictines and the Franciscans, but neither would satisfy me as to my own creative needs. I would ask, "What about my literary career? What about my capacity as a poet, my talents as a poet?" Each one told me that I would have to put that matter aside on entering. If in the decision of my superiors those talents were useful, well and good, but I could claim no mandate. Well, I could understand but couldn't accept it for myself. I knew the necessity to write was too deeply founded in me to renounce.

When my Guggenheim year came to a close in the spring of 1951, I applied for an extension, which was denied. I didn't want to go back to my job. Instead, I ended up in a Catholic Worker House of

Hospitality down on Skid Row in Oakland helping indigent men. But the real event there was meeting an ex-Trappist monk who taught me how to pray. He watched me for a week or so and finally approached me and said, "You aren't praying enough." "Why," I protested, "I pray three rosaries a day!" He said, "Three rosaries a day. That's nothing. That's chicken feed!" [*Laughter.*] So he said, "You follow me. You pray ten rosaries a day for ten days and I'll guarantee you results!" [*Laughter.*]

So I began to pray those ten rosaries a day. I did. I really began to bear down on those beads. Ten rosaries a day is a lot of prayer. But by golly, before those ten days were up we were praying fifteen and twenty rosaries a day. That's around eight solid hours of prayer. [*Laughter*] I took it on because I had read of the *Jesus Prayer* of the Russian pilgrims, repeating the holy name hour after hour as they walked. I mean we would walk around Skid Row jumbling those beads like a couple of idiots. I'd say "Hail Mary full of grace . . ." and he'd be right behind me with "Holy Mary Mother of God!" [*Laughter.*] The winos thought we had gone out of our heads.

Well, on the tenth day we went to mass that morning and I was almost sick with fatigue. But right out of the tabernacle came a bolt from the blue. I'm telling you it was my first great mystical experience, and the primary one. It hit me right in the heart like a sledgehammer. I went down like a poleaxed ox. I dropped in my pew and the tears poured down my face. It was so great, so beautiful. From that point on I knew. Up to then I had been searching, but from that point on I knew. And I still do. After twenty years nothing can erase the awful reality, the terrible truth of that experience.

Well, to get on with the story. On the strength of this experience the parish priest sent me to a Dominican. "This stuff," he said, "is too strong for me!"

[*Laughter.*] He never cottoned to all those rosaries in the first place.

The Dominican listened carefully and asked me a few questions. They were the right questions. When I answered as best I could, he nodded his head and said, "Yes, that's real. That's true." After a few months' work with him I began to read Dominican books. From them and from what I sensed in that Dominican priest, it began to dawn on me that maybe the Dominicans were where I belonged. But there still remained the problem of the literary career, and the poetic faculty.

He was dubious about my being a Dominican. I seemed too far out to fit into the local community at least. But he sent me to another priest, a theologian. When I asked him the telltale question about the talents he never batted an eye. "Of course you will develop your faculties," he said. "St. Thomas insists that the talents are God-given. I once had a superior who claimed that if the order accepted a man with a fine tenor voice it was obligated to develop it, even if it had to build him a soundproof room!" I stared at him in disbelief and exclaimed, "Let me in!" [*Laughter.*]

2

WE: The thrust toward handpress printing really began at Waldport when I found that even with Kalal's help I couldn't perfect the printing process. I wasn't enough of a mechanic. The mechanical press is a true machine, and I am not adept enough with machinery to produce the work I desired.

I remember reading somewhere that the printing device par excellence is the handpress, that the greatest books of modern times have been produced on it—the Kelmscott Press Chaucer, the Dove Press Bible, and the Ashenene Press Dante. Then too I knew of Eric Gill's work because my first wife was a sculptor, and among her collection she had Gill's books. Of these the most impressive was the *Autobiography*. I read there of the relation of printing to life, of a craft lived as a poetic vocation is lived.

When I came down to San Francisco on that furlough of 1944 I found a giant handpress in a printing equipment shop, a fantastic press. I cashed in an insurance policy to buy it and persuaded the shop owner to keep it for me till I could get released. Then I hauled it to Sebastopol and, as I said, back to Berkeley. I had me a press, but I had no idea how to make it work. That was something I had to learn from old printers' manuals.

Janitoring at the University of California I had

access to a great typographical library, Sam Farqu-
har's library. I'd get my work done early and go up
there and immerse myself in that library. The night
shift was good for me, because it allowed me to get
up in the morning fresh and plunge into either printing or writing. My janitor's shift ran from 4:00 P.M.
until midnight. That's the way I worked until the
Guggenheim came through.

DM: Did you carry the same press along with you
when you went into the Order?

WE: Yes. First I moved it down to Skid Row, though.
My Dominican guide insisted I had to resume my
craft, that I couldn't go on driving myself nuts with
all that prayer. When I entered the Order in 1951 I
moved the press to Saint Albert's and began to print
the *Psalter*.

JS: The *Psalter* is the major project?

WE: Yes.

DM: Did you translate the *Psalter* as well as print
it?

WE: Oh, no. I used the *Novum Psalterium PII XII*.
It was the first approved version of the psalms in
1,500 years and seemed like a great opportunity for
a printer.

JS: It's a beautiful piece of work. How many copies
did you do?

WE: I think forty-eight were bound. I tried for fifty.

DM: You didn't bind them yourself?

WE: No. I meant to. But when I abandoned it to try
for the priesthood, I sent the sheets to Dawson's
Bookshop in Los Angeles, who passed them on to
Mrs. Estelle Doheny, the great collector. She sent
them to the Lakeside Bindery in Chicago to be bound.
Some people say she must have paid seventy-five
dollars a copy to have them done.

DM: So you abandoned the project to go into the
priesthood?

WE: Yes.

DM: Were you finished with printing?

WE: No.

JS: So the bound *Psalter* is just a third of it?

WE: Right.

DM: What occurred when you decided to go into the priesthood?

WE: Well, when the novitiate period began in the fall of 1954 I went over to Kentfield and began the life of a clerical novice. This lasted six months. I blew up and went back to St. Alberts' in Oakland.

DM: When you say "blowing up," does that mean you couldn't endure within the structure?

WE: I couldn't maintain the regimen.

DM: What was it about the priesthood that you weren't able to contain within yourself?

WE: The emphasis on formal study. It was really the same reason I dropped out of college to become a poet. I couldn't master the formal intellectual application. The monastic life was the same. But for my writing and printing I now had to substitute study. Sheer unadulterated study. My psyche couldn't tolerate it after a while.

JS: How long was the proposed course of study?

WE: Seven years.

DM: During this period had you kept in contact with poets in the Bay Area?

WE: No. Rexroth and I had split. We had a falling out back in 1948, before I entered the Church. When I entered the Order, we were still out of communication.

DM: Were you in contact with any of the poets you knew earlier at Berkeley and at Waldport?

WE: Not during this period.

DM: When did you first meet Robert Duncan?

WE: I met Duncan way back before I went to camp. There was a magazine in Woodstock, New York, called the *Phoenix*, devoted to the memory of D. H. Lawrence. It was my interest in Lawrence that led me to send a contribution there. Duncan was in Woodstock with Sanders Russell beginning another magazine, the *Experimental Review*, and he saw my contribution and wrote to me. I responded and when Duncan returned to California he came down the Valley and dropped in for a visit with Edna and me on the farm. This was when I still had the land.

DM: He came on to settle in Berkeley?

WE: Yes, he studied at Cal.

JS: Did you know Mary Fabilli?

WE: He did but I didn't. He introduced me to Mary Fabilli's painting before I ever met her. I bought a drawing of hers and I had it on my wall long before I ever knew her.

DM: She designed his first book, *Heavenly City, Earthly City*.

WE: Mary did the illustrations for it. But that was after I was with her. We were in our most intensely sexual period, and that's why her rendition of Apollo in the cover illustration turned out to be so nakedly strong.

DM: What were the aspects of D. H. Lawrence's work that attracted you?

WE: The affinity to nature, and the celebration of sex as the central archetype of the natural. The first great impact in my creative life was Jeffers, the celebration of nature as divine, the divine made concrete, a kind of agonization of divinity in the concreteness of natural forms, what I would rather recognize as incarnation. Then in 1937 someone, some friend, smuggled into the country a copy of *Lady Chatterley's Lover*. Lawrence delivered sexuality from the torment of Jeffers and sang of it in its joy. With this book I adopted him as my number two formative master. Both the Jeffers and Lawrence interests led me to Lawrence Clark Powell, and through Powell I encountered Henry Miller. All this before the war.

Powell told Miller about me, and he came up the Valley from Los Angeles with Gilbert Neiman and stayed at our house overnight. Edna and I had read all his books before we met him. They were quite unknown in this country except by hearsay. Powell had lent us his copies, until a Trotskyite seaman in Fresno named Carl smuggled in pirated editions from Hong Kong. As a revolutionary Carl repudiated my pacifist stand, but the poor devil was torpedoed in the Carribbean by a German U-boat and never seen again. I remember how impressed he was with the purity of Chinese whores. When they ganged up on you in port you could scatter them just by saying, "Suckee! Suckee!" But the first pirated edition of *Black Spring* that Miller ever saw was a copy Carl got for me.

DM: Was Miller's work influential?

WE: Not in any stylistical way. What Miller taught me was . . . how shall I put it? Not just the desirability, but the *necessity* of going-for-broke. And not just in the aesthetic sense.

With both Jeffers and Lawrence there was always the primacy of the aesthetic. Traditional ·literary values were used to orient the mind into violational areas, sexual explicitness subsumed in the aesthetic intuition. Miller taught me the truth of going-for-broke even without the blessing of the aesthetic. Just the raw force of language humping you through, that preaesthetic draft into the unconscious, the sexual surcharge lifted out of the pornographic, not by aesthetics as other writers had done, but by the naked energy invested in language itself. That alone. I never attempted it for myself, but at last I began to realize what was possible. With those three masters behind me I was set up for the work I had to do.

JS: You met Lawrence Clark Powell through your interest in Jeffers, or your interest in printing?

WE: The Jeffers interest, before the printing. I read

Powell's book on Jeffers, then a mutual friend sent him my poems, and we began to correspond. . . . But our relation was one of sharing inner thoughts rather than of stylistic influence or derivation either way. We corresponded monumentally.

DM: It's interesting that Miller wrestled with Lawrence's work and tried to write a book on him and failed, whereas Anaïs Nin, who figures importantly in Miller's formative time in Paris, wrote an excellent study on Lawrence.

WE: I never read that.

DM: She perceives Lawrence and his work as a woman, and it is the feminine responsiveness to it that makes her book so valuable.

WE: I met Anaïs Nin and felt very attracted to her— a beautiful woman. Did you know that Duncan was once her secretary? They quarreled, however. When I met her she was so furious with Robert she wouldn't speak to him.

Duncan was often difficult in those days. He is mellower now; success has made him more secure. But when he wanted to, he could be a real son of a bitch. (I say this affectionately.) But he was so childlike, so childish, that you just had to make allowances for him and accept his friendship for what it was. When he became insecure in a group he would try to overcome it by talking above his head. Voice raised. Eyes dilated. He would expatiate in the most astonishing way. Often he was brilliant, but other times he would soon have hardly any friends left in the room. But I always admired him as a comrade and friend, and I always believed in him as a poet. Because he is a lovable person.

JS: Were you seeing him and having literary contacts outside the monastery?

WE: No. I wasn't seeing Duncan at all. He'd gone on to Black Mountain, I think, following Olson there. I met Charles Olson in 1947. He came out here to the

West Coast with his first wife. I believe *Call Me Ishmael* was just out. He was looking for another project and was going to the Sierras to check out the area where the Donner party starved to death. But it didn't turn out. His wife went back East and he stayed out here for a winter.

There's a story regarding Olson and me. He came to our house one night and waited for me to come back from my swing-shift janitor job. Charles chucklingly recalls that in the middle of the night, when I finally got home, I had to take my wife upstairs first thing and get laid before I could come back down and be sociable.

Well, in the first place I simply wouldn't be capable of that. What really happened was he arrived hoping for a spot for the night and Mary Fabilli was quite uptight with him. He's an enormous man, you know, a whale of a man, and they sat there eyeing one another. He's a lapsed Catholic and Mary was already gung-ho about Catholicism, struggling back to the faith, and all. I don't know what he said that got her going. But anyway, when I arrived home she was upset. And her Maybeck house doesn't have any privacy, really. The whole lower floor is built so you can hear everything in every room. So Mary gave me the high sign and led me upstairs to the bedroom. "Get him out of here," she told me. "I can't stand the man!" It was by then one o'clock in the morning and I know Charles had no place to go, but I had to tell him that I was sorry. Women are like that. Bleeding hearts over a wounded bird, but with their husband's cronies they can be flint. Poor Charles shambled off into the night. But I wouldn't be capable of making out, like he thinks I did, not with a friend waiting downstairs.

DM: Did you have any contact with Patchen during that time?

WE: We did a book of his with Untide at Waldport

during the war. *An Astonished Eye Looks Out of The Air,* his antiwar poetry. We had difficulties, the relationship broke, and I never had much to do with him after that. It wasn't until 1960 or so that I met him in Seattle, and we were friendly, I'm glad to say.

Duncan had warned me that Kenneth Patchen is the poet little presses fold on. You begin with having a Patchen book as a wonderful prospect. The next thing you know he's breathing down your collar. And suddenly he's reaching over your shoulder. It's impossible.

Jack Stauffacher once started a book with Patchen. Jack is a meticulous printer and likes to proceed at a reflective pace. He thought he had an understanding with a genial poet that would make an interesting project to do. But he hadn't got on very far with it when the door would open and this figure would be standing there with accusing eyes. "How are you coming with my book . . .?"

But I do believe in Patchen's witness. I don't cotton to his poetry the way I do that of Rexroth and Duncan. But I do believe in his witness.

3

DM: You were one of the first poets I heard when I came to San Francisco. They were having an arts festival in North Beach and there were readings at Fugazi Hall during the day. You were reading with some other poets and I remember you had a black suit on. The hall was relatively empty and we were all sitting on wooden benches. I remember I was listening for the sound of what poetry should be. And I remember the impact and power of your reading, even though, at that time, I had never heard of you.

I remember I came to San Francisco to seek my poetic identity and found a lot of people just sitting around. Not the archetype, but the stereotype media created in multitudes. What did emerge at that time was the rise of poetry into more of a public art . . . the poet as spokesman, the poet as conscience, as well as the poet as entertainer.

WE: Exactly. That's why I always identified with the Beat Generation—the point you're making just now. I'd never let any kind of negative aura around the beat image deter me from the primacy of that fact. It put poetry back on the platform. We had been trying for a whole decade to get something like the Beat Generation going. We tried it back in the late forties with Rexroth, and were successful enough to get attacked in *Harper's*, as "The New Cult of Sex and Anarchy." But the nation as a whole wasn't ready for it, what with the postwar preoccupation and the cold-war freeze. It took Korea and the second Eisenhower administration to make the country ready. It took the man in the gray flannel suit as the national image and the crew cut as the prevailing college mode. The tranquilized fifties. I remember that *Life* magazine titled its big feature on the beats *The Only Rebellion Around,* almost begging for dissent. Now they've got their belly full of it.

As I say, out here in San Francisco we were ready for it long before the rest of the country, but we couldn't have pulled it off alone. It took something outside ourselves, something from the East Coast to make a true *conjuntio oppositorium,* a conjunction of the opposites. As it turned out Allen Ginsberg and Jack Kerouac provided the ingredients. They came to San Francisco and found themselves, and it was *their* finding that sparked *us*. Without them, it would never have happened.

DM: What made you emerge from seven years of a rather closely regimented monastic life?

WE: I was called out, really. The Beat Generation broke with the second issue of the *Evergreen Review*, the feature that announced the San Francisco renaissance. Our poems were there, but more importantly our photographs were there. Harry Redl's portfolio of portraits was added to that issue almost as an afterthought, but in my opinion it made the issue. It's astonishing how a photographer's point of view can give to a group a collective identity it doesn't actually possess. I'd never even met Ginsberg or Kerouac, but under Redl's somber lens we all looked like brothers. Soon requests for readings began to come in. My superiors would evaluate each one on its own merits, then give me the permission to take it. And actually it wasn't the readings that got me in trouble, it was the interviews.

JS: How was that?

WE: Well, the image of a Roman Catholic religious poet as an exponent of the beat generation was sensational enough to attract the press. It was this image more than anything I actually said that set the hierarchy's teeth on edge. After the *Time* feature on me in 1959, the archbishop lowered the boom. I'll never forget *him*. John J. Mitty, Archbishop of San Francisco. His clergy didn't call his "Cactus Jack" for nothing.

DM: You mean he silenced you?

WE: He tried to. He silenced me locally and tried to silence me nationally. My superiors had to go along with his wishes as far as his own diocese was concerned, and they began to be more choosy about where I could read. They made me stop giving interviews to the press. And they denied me the use of the religious habit on platform. Lord, I suffered during this period. I thought they should stand up and fight him, but they said they couldn't possibly win on an issue like that. I submitted. Within a couple of years he was dead and the ban was lifted. I saw his death as divine retribution. [*Laughter.*] But I had a beautiful Mexican friend named Rose who saw it otherwise. Unshakably loyal to both the charismatic and institutional aspects of the Church, she declared: "This lifting of the ban proves that his grace is already in heaven and moving to correct the natural mistakes of his episcopate!" [*Laughter.*] Meantime we had a new provincial also. The ban was lifted and I was back on platform, interviews, religious habit, and all.

DM: It must have been unusual to leave that closed life and find yourself on the platform with people you hadn't seen for seven years.

WE: In the beginning all I could do was just get up there and lose myself in the voice, let the voice itself carry me through. That's what you heard in Fugazi Hall.

JS: How did this influence your poetry? Did it happen to occur at a time when you needed something?

WE: Well, the poetry had dried up, all right, but that was in the novitiate studying for the priesthood. *The Crooked Lines of God* was finished there in 1954 and I didn't write again until 1957. It was the crystallized monastic ego that dried the poetry out of me. Heap big monk. I had no way through until the summer of 1956 when I underwent a real psychic break, a real invasion of the unconscious. This took me into depth psychology. Out of this inner break, almost as a lifesaving thing, the poetry began to flow.

JS: What do you mean by depth psychology?

WE: Jung. I began to study Jung. I took up the

analysis of dreams. The years between 1956 and 1960 were spent primarily on dream analysis. At the same time I was writing *The Hazards of Holiness*. But the main force of my thought was in depth psychology, in dream analysis. Jung was the master who showed me the way through that.

DM: It seems your creative cycles are always led by a master, a guide.

WE: That's right. When I need knowledge the masters always appear to guide me. But in terms of instinctual impasse the guide is usually a woman.

DM: How about some of the younger poets here in 1959? Did you get to know any of them well?

WE: No, I wish I had. But my image of a monk was such that when we occasionally met we were never really free with each other. The fault was mine. As you say, to come out from so many years of monasticism wasn't easy. My first meeting with Allen Ginsberg was not a happy one. In those days he used to come up to anyone having a religious orientation and open with, "Have you had any mystical experiences?" I shouldn't have let it turn me off, but I couldn't be so free about such matters.

I'll always remember a story about Allen seeking across India for the absolute guru. Finally he found this ragged holy man, half gone with visionary rapture, sitting by a path in the lotus position. Allen rushed up to him and in broken Hindu stammered: "O Master! I have come all the way across the ocean to find you! Tell me, have you experienced the *Paranirvana*, the nirvana beyond nothingness?" The old adept opened his eyes and focused them blankly on Allen for a long moment. Then he replied in perfect English: "None of your fucking business!"

That's really unfair. Allen Ginsberg is one of the crystallizing forces of this time. His poem *Howl* remains what Rexroth first called it: "The confessions of faith of a new generation." Few people yet grasp how so much of what is happening now goes back to the writing of a poem in the Drake Hotel cafeteria on Powell Street in San Francisco.

4

WE: It was in 1963, after twelve years in the Order, that I finally returned to Kentfield Priory to begin my novitiate as a lay brother. You see, I entered the Dominicans as a donatus or oblate, as the Benedictines term it: a monk without vows. This was because my previous marriage constituted a canonical impediment to profession, to vows taking. I immediately petitioned the Order for a dispensation but they asked me to wait. I kept trying, though. I must have petitioned four or five times all through the fifties.

DM: And did they continue to refuse?

WE: The first two provincials did, and I quit trying. Then a new provincial in 1960 came to me and said, "Antoninus, you've earned your spurs. You've had ten years on a broom. I'm going to take you off that and let you do your own thing." So finally I was free to devote my entire time to writing and the poetry-reading circuit, which was cresting then as a big thing on the campuses. This is why I stopped petitioning them on the matter of vows. It was pointed out to me that had I been in vows they probably would not have allowed me so much liberty.

It was about this time that I met Rose and began

to write *The Rose of Solitude*. She had been born
Rose Moreno in Austin, Texas. She married very
young, one of those German Catholic Texans, and
ended up in San Francisco, divorced, with three
children. I met her through a friend in the Order and
she began to come to me for counseling. But the
situation reversed very fast. I fell in love with her,
and placed my life in her hands, so to speak. That's
not so unusual a thing as it seems, actually. St.
Catherine of Siena and St. Teresa of Avila were each
the spiritual advisers to many priests and religious.
I had had a rift with Mary Fabilli after she rejected
an autobiography I had written. The Order said she
had to approve it before it could be published, and
she refused. It caused a break between us, left me
hanging, so to speak . . .

DM: Why did she refuse?

WE: Deeply personal reasons. Ortega y Gasset says
it's the nature of man to express his intuitions, the
nature of woman to contain them.

JS: You mean you have a completed autobiography
that's never been published, and can't be published?

WE: It's just as well. It was too apologetical, really,
and after Vatican II that emphasis went out. But to
get on, Rose brought a new dimension into my life,
a new version of woman. Beautiful and ardent and
adamant, she took over after Mary and for five years
my life was hers. Not that Mary was not beautiful
and ardent and adamant in her own right. She was
and is. But Mary is an Italian and an artist, while
Rose is a Mexican and a mystic—an altogether more
primitive sensibility, capable of fanatical Mexican
asceticism, spikes in the flesh, that sort of thing. Yet
with an overlay of sophistication that was like nothing I had ever experienced. She never missed daily
mass, but her perfume was My Sin!

I did not introduce her into the literary life around

San Francisco, even though I was now moving through it again. It had been my world with Mary Fabilli, and I wanted to learn Rose's world. Oh, I took her to one of Kenneth Rexroth's annual birthday parties, and she was sensational there. And I once took Phil Whalen and Don Carpenter by her house and basked in the effect she created. But her meaning in my life lay elsewhere, and I prefer to keep these things separate.

For as I say she led me out into that world of café society which I had never known, had feared and disdained. She was preparing me for the cocktail rounds every poet has to survive as a literary lion on the lecture circuit. After the red wine of the bohemian period, I learned to drink Scotch and daiquiris. And she taught me the art of holding a contemplative life in the midst of the social whirl, the mystic encounter with people in a highly transitory social milieu, how to go the limit until you collapse, then bounce back and keep moving, keep swinging. Rose is a swinger, and watching her I saw how it's done.

Then in 1963, out of the blue, she told me the time had come for me to petition again to take vows. This threw me. I did not want to forfeit the freedom I had gained so arduously in the Order, and besides I was cresting at that time on the poetry-reading circuit and I wanted to keep hammering away while the iron was hot. I had had too many instances in my career of changing course just on the threshold of a real triumph. But Rose was adamant. The request was granted immediately—an instance of her mystic intuition. That fall I found myself off the lecture circuit and back in the novitiate at Kentfield, locked up.

That was the end. When you leave a woman's life you leave a vacuum behind you, and somebody's going to fill it. It happened with Edna when I was drafted. It happened with Mary when I entered the

Order—though in her case I was not supplanted by another lover but by a father confessor. And now it happened with Rose.

The thing about Rose is that once a man goes out of her life, she never turns back. It's that stone knife in the Aztec heart, that Capricorn heart. I saw it happen with others and I knew when it happened to me. You know, in my horoscope I have an afflicted moon. The interpretation is that the women in your life will always somehow fail you, and sure enough, they have. But each has brought me a new kind of realization that I needed, so it's not really a matter of failure. A man has to make his defeats with women the building stones of his perfection.

So at Kentfield I found myself on my own again. When the novitiate period was over and my first vows pronounced, I hit the road. Rather than sending me back to Oakland I was kept stationed in Kentfield as home base. Then in 1968 they sent all us lay brothers back to St. Albert's as part of a new policy.

DM: What is the difference between the priesthood studies that you undertook at Kentfield ten years before and the studies you took on as a lay brother novice when you arrived in 1963?

WE: Well, the lay brother novitiate these days is the same as that of the clerical novitiate, but at that time they were different. The lay brother novitiate then was still largely a period of learning to live the monastic life through prayer and work. That's why it was unfair to send me back after being in the Order for twelve years. They could easily have got a dispensation for me. They'd done it with other oblates before me.

JS: Do you know why they didn't?

WE: Well, they said that having petitioned Rome for one dispensation, my marital dispensation, they did not want to press their luck with a second one. But that really doesn't figure. I think it's some kind of archetypal suspicion of the poet, the distrust of the cleric for the poet. When I left the Order, the president of St. Albert's explained to the press that I was always more the poet than the theologian. Almost as if to say, "We told you so."

DM: Were there any beneficial characteristics in those two disruptions?

WE: Yes, the overall result was clarifying and resolving. You never know if you're meant for a thing until you've tried it, and even if it doesn't prove out, there's an inner liberation, as of something settled or confirmed. I was happy at Kentfield after St. Albert's. It's a smaller house, and more removed. There's more nature there, Marin County is heaven after Oakland! I was in a better position to live out the loss of Rose, a better place to lick my wounds. And it was there, in 1965, that I met Sue, Some will say cynically, "On the rebound," but rebounds don't last. If they last they're not mere rebounds. And I gave this one four years before I trusted it. So you can't call it a rebound. Anyway, at Kentfield the new fate began. I can see by hindsight that the ground was being laid for my transition out of the Order.

DM: Is it true, that in the week between your leaving the Order and your formal marriage to Sue, Rose showed up at Stinson Beach to dissuade you from it, to make you return to the Order?

WE: She did.

JS: Would you care to talk about that?

WE: No.

5

DM: During all these disruptions you were spending a great deal of time on the reading circuit. How did you regard that experience?

WE: I regard it always as a witness. On the college campuses the emphasis is on communication, what you know. I can communicate, but the witness is greater. It's something like this: what you can communicate maintains the point of contact, but it isn't the essence of your total effect, which is witness. By witness I mean a personal confrontation, a personal encounter, a psychic crisis deliberately precipitated to produce a change in attitude, a new center of gravity, a displacement of consciousness from cognition to faith. I don't mean faith in the Catholic sense. I never proselytize. I mean faith in the sense of commitment to life and to living. To live my faith, rather than by the mental thing that our education inculcates. To enter via the ideational world, yes, but to move through it. To be able to field the questions as they come to you and at the same time to throw back into the questioner a different principle of life. We are familiar with this from the example of the Zen masters, but my point of orientation is not Zen.

The Beat Generation began it back in 1959. And it took, you know, it really took. It took more than any of us thought possible. Certainly the image took. The credit is usually given the Beatles, but the Beatles can't be compared with the beats. They were the middlemen between the beats and the rising generation, because the beats alone could never make that image all that popular. Nevertheless it began in a different place, another point in the psychic hemisphere. Not Liverpool but San Francisco.

JS: Is the platform also a testing ground?

WE: Not really. I never considered it that way. The testing ground was back in the monastic cell, where the interiority of vision was fought out and preserved. The testing ground was in the writing of the poem, not its utterance on platform. Once you are on platform you have to be absolute master or you're lost. The long periods of withdrawal build, they build fantastically. They fill you up, and you move out into the world. And at the point of contact, the crucial issue, you respond. It's not that you have it programmed like a good debater, all the answers, etc. It isn't that at all. It's just that when the point of issue actually occurs you are there to meet it. And you do meet it. Because you know what you are. There isn't any other principle, really, than that.

For me, this will go on. It's not something that will end with my change of life. True, I learned it in the monastery. I learned what it is, the meaning of it, and its tremendous value. From the monastery I brought out to the world an image consonant with its essence: the religious habit, the robes. But now that the robes are gone, the same thing will go forward, and in going forward a new image will emerge. I don't know what it will be. I won't know until the first encounter.

The monastic life gives you terrific capacity for reflection. There is awesome power in it. Separation from the world really constitutes a kind of power. I'm sure that the orders are by no means finished. It's just that so few in the orders ever discover how to utilize the power they possess. The shift in Western culture from a religious orientation to a secular orientation has left them in a kind of backwash, and they haven't been able to free themselves because their parochial constituency prefer them as fixated security symbols in a transient world rather than moving and living dynamic charismatic entities. As a brother, I really feel that I perfected the accommodation of that religious power to the point of issue in the world of today. Perhaps that's why I left. As someone has said, "What you've perfected, you've condemned."

As I look back on it . . . and I hope I'm no bragging, only just musing about something that is no more . . . it seems my approach was an almost perfect equation between the monastic life (the principle of reflection) and the point of application that youth was asking for on the campus. If it wasn't absolutely perfect, it was because it took so long to perfect it—ten, twelve years. As you yourself saw me there in the beginning, in Fugazi Hall in 1958, it was so utterly stark. There was no point of mediation except the primal voice of the poet. But after awhile I began to orient myself.

I'm just wondering what's going to happen now. This great break that I've made, I can't justify it. Not in terms of my Catholic beliefs. But I feel God has something in store for me that I could not accomplish in the context of the Order. What it is I don't know. It remains to be discovered.

DM: You were inside the monastic life for sixteen years?

WE: Eighteen, almost nineteen years. Even though I was out of the monastery a good deal on reading tours, nevertheless the monk was always there. What's going to happen to the monk?

I find there are two different worlds, the domestic world and the monastic world, with the prophetic role bearing the same relation to each. The domestic world is much taken up with trivia, and the Church ranks the monastic life higher because its detachment from trivia renders it so accessible to spiritual infusion. But it seems to me that once the domestic life, the life of trivia, is constituted as a permeable reflective form, then the prophetic role, the poet's role, may draw on it with the same accessibility as it does on the monastic life. What I'm saying is that, monasticism or domesticity, the prophetic function must go on.

Yet it's difficult, for I don't know the world, really. I don't know how much money you need to live, to get by on. I don't know anything about that. And I don't know where to throw my energies in terms of it. Before the Order I was able to constitute the domestic life as a permeable reflective form, but I had no children. Very likely that was the reason I feared children, why I became a monk. But now I have a boy to raise to manhood. So the life of a parent, the life of responsibility in trivia, confronts me.

DM: Do you plan to continue your reading tours?

WE: Well, I announced that I was going to stop for a while, but my agent asked me to keep going, to honor the contracts I had already signed.

DM: You'll now be reading without your religious habit?

WE: Yes.

JS: Will you read in your black suit?

WE: I don't know. Sue doesn't want me to get into that black suit again!

JS: It would be interesting to see you reading in buckskin or corduroy.

WE: I'd like to wear buckskin. But it just seems like too much. It's the Virgo in me that hesitates to go that far. But Virgo has to learn to jump through its own shadow, and maybe that's what I will eventually do.

JS: What made you announce that you were going to stop reading?

WE: Taste as much as anything. That and the natural reluctance to exploit a denial of all you stood for. It would seem to require an absolute break. Also in order to go through a period of silence and withdrawal to prepare for a new phase. I think all great things should be prepared for by a period of withdrawal. I really feel that. But not seven years . . .! [*Laughter.*] Actually, I'm ready to go back on platform. I can tell by talking tonight that I truly am.

JS: David and I have many times talked about Lew Welch's once proposed magazine, *Bread*. It was planned to present a variety of esays and poems dealing with the poet's considerations about trivia—about how to get along, how to pay the bills, how to keep the lights turned on, the children fed, the wife happy. It's interesting to hear of your encountering these problems after having them somewhat solved for you.

WE: Yes, in the monastic life everything is provided for you. That's the great thing about it, but also the reason why so many lay people call it a cop-out. What they don't see is that you pay plenty for it in terms of restrictions, and that these restrictions are the prime ingredient in enforcing the interiority that is the purpose of the life. Anyone who thinks the monastic life is a cop-out is welcome to go and try it. He'll find out.

Actually, in the monastery I went my own way as a writer. It took ten years on the broom before I was free to rove as a lecturer, but that kind of submission eventually proves that. In the end I had it like no one else: free to write, free to lecture. I can hear someone say, "Yeah, and he hung himself. They gave him enough rope and he hung himself." I guess I did, but the process was a true working-out.

DM: How do you find the world?

WE: Tough. I'm still smarting from my break, and I

dare say I'm not yet seeing things as they actually are. A routine dental appointment came up last week, one I'd made while still in the Order. I've known this dentist for fifteen years. I hesitated to go back there after my break, but it seemed cowardice not to, since he knows my teeth inside out, and put a lot of time into them free of charge. He is a conservative, a Republican, an ex-navy man, a staunch Catholic, and I knew he would be offended at my leaving the Order. But I also thought it was something we could talk about. I should have sensed something from the receptionist's attitude, but I was totally unprepared when he emerged in the sitting room and announced in front of the others waiting there: "For my own reasons, I don't want you for my patient!"

One of the fondest items of liberal polemics is that of the clergy as a high-placed nucleus maintaining position at the laity's expense. Actually the laity invests fantastic emotional security in the image of the priest and the nun, fixating them in rigid personas and denying them the full ambience of their humanity. The gun at the head of the clergy is the crushing burden of responsibility thrust upon them by these "little ones." Anyone who has seen pictures of the pope being mobbed by weeping, pleading supplicants, grown men and women who touch his robes and kiss his hands, can see what every priest is up against, and every monk and nun, too.

In the spring of 1968 I took Susanna to my favorite restaurant in San Francisco, the Tadish Grill. It was on this occasion that she told me she had fallen in love with a young man who had recently taken lodging at her rooming house, and who in the course of impending events was to become the father of little Jude. She was so radiant and daughterly that I could only rejoice for her. Although I was in mufti at the time, it so happened that I was recognized by an entering family of Catholics—no one I knew, but the fact of recognition was evident. Normally, I would have conducted myself prudently, but in view of what Sue had just told me, and since it was apparent that this occasion was to be one of farewell, I would not think of being anything less than true to the state of poignancy and relinquishment we were experiencing. So I took her hand and gazed, with all the meaning I could muster, into her eyes as we shared that meal. The Catholics were disturbed. They stared at me disapprovingly, in fact, incredulously. Yet we did nothing wrong. It was only that I had violated the convention of how a celibate is expected to act publicly. At the bottom it is the Catholic laity who provide for the sustenance of the monk, and they let you know if your need for latitude conflicts with their need for security, with its heavy investment in your decorum.

DM: Have you had the opposite kind of reaction: have you had people welcome you with open arms?

WE: Very much. The response from that quarter has been gratifying. Sometimes not too much understanding of what you put into it and what it cost you to go. I find myself disturbed by people who exclaim, "Welcome back!"

Tina: Has anybody said, "Where have you been!" [*Laughter.*]

WE: Actually, it's more the practical problem of how to restructure your life on a daily basis after so many years of monasticism. The problem of adjusting to the child has been a big one. If it were just the erotic relationship . . . I've been through that before. But when a child comes into it, every time you make love, there's a third person to consider.

DM: How old is he?

WE: Ten months.

DM: Are there any problems of making a living at the moment?

WE: Sue has an income, so that's not the main problem right now. I can supplement it, of course. One reason I must get back on the road and carry my own share, as they say. I've begun a new sequence of poems, and they should be ready by fall.

DM: You must have imagined at times, in the monastery, being out, didn't you?

WE: Yes, but not seriously. I had every expectation of ending my days in the Order. Even after finding myself in love, I didn't want to give up that image of the monk. That was the hardest thing, because I had perfected it, and knew how to use it. Not that I didn't live the monastic life, I did in the beginning, I used to crawl back from being on tour as a hermit crawls back to his cave. But eventually I learned how to keep my spiritual balance, even on the road. Rose taught me that. But what I didn't want to give up was my pride, my image. Oh, the sweet power in that image!

By leaving it I did, though only a woman could have dragged me from it. That was the most terrible thing to forsake, that beautiful image, that beautiful habit and the power in it. I know this sounds power-thirsty, and I won't minimize it. But if you're a prophet and have not completed your work in the world, to relinquish a power you have perfected in order to start all over again is terrible.

6

WE: I distinguish between the poem written and the poem read. The poem read is the confrontation with the world, but the poem written is the confrontation with the self, the unknown part of the self, which is hidden. This is carried on at an entirely different level than the blazing confrontation which the world exacts. We begin as introverts, the reason why so many poets are poor readers. For the art of the platform is an art of extroversion. You master the problem by throwing a more challenging confrontation back to the world than it is prepared for. This enables you to survive even as you insist on your own terms. For this reason I will sometimes outrageously exploit my poems when I read. Whereas when I write, it is as private a thing as my love life. There is all the privacy of the bedroom about it. Procreation and insemination. Except that the dialogue is with the self, the unknown self. In the act of creation we find the pagan in ourself, the primitive. We find *him*, or *her*, or *it*—whatever it is that has not yet yielded to formality.

And it taunts us, and rebukes us, mocking us with the limitation of formality, suffering itself to be accepted only under the most specifically appropriate terms. And so the poem emerges, the ritual in which the dialogue with the mysterious self is consummated.

These truths are weapons. I have this knowledge, this secret knowledge. And it is the knowledge that enables me to confront the world, convert my intro- version into a true extroversion. What I have achieved is irreducible. No one can take it from me. Nothing that happens out there can nullify it.

And the heart of encounter, as I said, is witness. Witness is the passion that propels me, as monk or citizen. A man is seldom honored for that. The world wants to be entertained. You have honored me when you spoke of the primacy of the voice at that Fugazi Hall reading, but a poet can take an audience to the depths and have it spit in his face. That is what being a prophet means. No performer alive can hold such power over a people, for the poet is the archetype of the performer. But that power brings pain. Any psy- chiatrist, any counselor or confessor, will tell you the same thing. A psychiatrist will wait weeks for the moment he can truthfully tell what he has truthfully discerned. The patient leaves his office exalted with a kind of received wisdom. But the next day he is back glaring and muttering accusations. "Human kind," as Eliot has said, "cannot bear very much real- ity." The same thing goes for your audience. You can shake them to the bone, move them with a religious revelation they never before experienced. But the responses the next day are mixed, and the reviews, if you are lucky enough to get any, say "excessive" or "emotional." Or they speak of the performance as "uneven." Uneven! Good God! I seek perfection, in my life and in my craft, but I will jeopardize it if need be, and sometimes sacrifice it deliberately, in order to touch, to move, to change attitudes, con- front lives. This is the meaning of witness.

"Ah yes," the critic replies, "but it is not art!" I deny the distinction. In his *Essays on the Philosophy of Art,* Collingwood spells it out: "The artist must prophesy not in the sense that he foretells things to come, but in the sense that he tells his audience, at the risk of their displeasure, the secrets of their own hearts."

I have emphasized the prophetic role of the poet because of the relevance of the prophet's moral confrontation as it derives from our Old Testament heritage. But now that I'm out of the Order and experiencing the recovery of nature (not so much probing it as letting it invade me), I feel that those young San Francisco poets who localize the matter in the image of the shaman are closer to the truth for our time. The more you study the function of the shaman as archetypal creator and poet—as seen, for instance, in those fantastic bison preserved for us in the Altamira caves: figures replete with that unbelievable delicacy of abstraction that could only have come from sources of the utmost psychic cruciality (even if, unfortunately, the performance was "uneven"!). A function brought right up to our own times in the tribes out here on the coast, for whom the shaman served as tribal psychic stabilizer, as well as master of ecstasy in the dance and the peyote cult. So I am becoming more aware of the deepening relevance of the shaman for our time, and the poet's archaic connection with him. In fact, come to think of it, the first time I ever read the term was in Duncan's poem *Toward the Shaman,* printed in the *Experimental Review* before the war.

And the more I reflect on what actually happens on platform, the more I am convinced it is shamanistic rather than prophetic—the trancelike rhythms, the unspeakable silences, the incredible psychic polarization in the audience—these are all ingredients of the shamanistic syndrome. Of course, this function has now been largely taken over by the rock band. The infusion of oriental tonalities into rock in the sixties is the clearest indication of its appropriation of the shamanistic role. We beats were a manifestly poetry-oriented generation, whereas the voice of the succeeding one is indubitably rock, so that poetry is relatively unemphasized right now. I think this is to be expected, while the implications of rock are being extended. But this does not mean that the place of poetry has been altered. Pure tonality augments, but does not supplant the primacy of concept, for it is founded on the priority of inception: "In the beginning was the Word . . ." I believe that in the field of expression, music emerged and developed as an augmentation and extension of the Word's latent nuance's which poetry's limited tonalities of necessity could not articulate. Sometimes the Word must retire in order to let these latencies find their activation. But it can never be a matter of primacy. I have experienced too much on platform to fear that any music can usurp the poet's place in the field of man's awareness. For his verse clinches the point of cognition, the bone-cold nucleus in the vast connotative flux. What poetry concedes to music in the area of the implicit is more than recovered in the area of the explicit, where music never can challenge it.

Anyway, it's this consideration, this complex of considerations, that makes me feel the transposition from the religious habit to, say, buckskin, if that's the way I am meant to go, has an unconscious validation that authenticates it as something more than affectation. The deep work now confronting man is to touch the roots of his symbolic motivation. It was shaman's work once and it is the poet's work now, and it will be met.

Thinking of this struggle, I remember that I listened to you both read on the same program at Santa Barbara a little less than a year ago. David, I could see, had had more experience on platform, and had through pain been liberated into a direct feeling-rapport, a true discursive, with the audience. Whereas you, Jack, had not had so much exposure. The audience had not yet clarified you and purified you through the suffering of your prophetic witness as poet, or I should say your shamanistic witness. For the shaman this purification was done in solitude, immersal in the wilderness. The wilderness was then man's problem, and deliverance comes only from being swallowed up by your problem, like Jonah in the whale's belly. But it is increasingly evident that such solitude is no longer feasible, for the wilderness is no longer man's problem, except how to preserve it.

What is truly his problem today is the wilderness of the race itself, the vast, anonymous, terrifying, and inscrutable population that everywhere surrounds us, and which for the poet is symbolized by his audience. For him, paradoxically, the solitude and the suffering are undergone on platform.

I know this contradicts what I said earlier in answer to your question of whether or not platform constitutes a testing. I was struck cold by the realization that the platform is too late for testing. It is the arena. And yet so was the wilderness for the shaman. The platform for the poet, like the wilderness for the shaman, is not a place of testing. It is a place of survival. For me, my testing was my solitude, and my solitude was my cell, and that solitude formed me. And yet that is nothing compared to the terrible solitude, the isolation one undergoes on platform. I think it is crucial to see the audience as the active force, the dangerous unconscious force. Then the audience as the bull and the poet the matador. Until you have been gored a few times, your vocation has not been confirmed. We wait always for the baptism of blood. In her book *Waiting for God* Simone Weil quotes with approval the saying of French craftsmen, that until an apprentice has been hurt by his tools, "the craft has not yet entered into his body."

DM: Your view, then, that in his platform role the poet accommodates to a persona, or mask, which in your case the religious habit confirmed and which, as you say, the transposition might well extend—this is a different thing, as you have indicated, than the creation of the poem itself.

WE: Actually, I believe that in every response, the psychic element we designate as the persona is in play, that it is not only an indispensable factor in the creative process but in the psychic process itself. It complicates, but in some strange way it precipitates cognition. Among the implicit criteria of sanctity in our time, the one that presupposes a totally unstructured awareness, pure spontaneity responding without inhibition or equivocation or any suggestion of predetermination. Thus I have heard Allen Ginsberg called "our only modern saint" because of his apparent liberation from our collective taboos. But this assumption is one of our myths; insofar as it is entertained as an ethos or value it is itself memorialized as a constitutive persona. Let's say that the persona is the ineluctable concomitant of concept, which is attitude. Persona is the prism through which subjective attitude is conferred on objective reality. It is only objectionable when it is not really one's own. The poet might as well accept its presence as something given, something ineradicably present in the creation of his poem.

It's harder to speak of what happens in the writing than what happens on platform, because in the writing everything is introjected. The creation of a poem is like a love word uttered; you are not aware that you have spoiled it until it is too late. If when you speak to your beloved you are unsure, it is implicitly revealed in the signature of the inflection. Then you find trueness in yourself, maybe out of your experience, certainly out of your suffering, always, if you do, the grace of God, and the uttered word comes true, not a quiver of uncertainty . . . and you and your beloved understand each other. So it is also with the writing of the poem, only the achievement is permanent.

This makes it terrible. From one point of view it is horribly like photographing your beloved in the moment of giving herself to you. Who would do that? Yet as a poet you do it. Except we deal with more intangible forms.

For there is this inscrutable character of the language, its capacity to both withhold and manifest at the same time. This is so strange. Everything that happens in a poem happens in terms of language. You cannot exceed the language. You can never say more than it says. The collective nature of the language is the boundary you can never cross. Your personal language, yes, you can rattle off. The baby babbles. But the collective nature of language remains intransigent. You finally begin to realize that the other self—the *he* or *she* or the *it* whom you address —is your collective self. This mysterious one is really all men. We talk about it as the most deeply personal self, and so it seems. But who does it turn out to be? It turns out to be the race! This is the explanation of craftsmanship, and why it works, why it is necessary. It liberates the impersonal through efficiency. But if it is merely effectual it's like the lover who is merely skilled. Who ever heard of an efficient lover?

This is why it's easy to write the first poem. A minimal craftsmanship is endowed in your tongue. The problem is how do you keep doing it. Again, it's like in love. It's easy to make love the first time. The act is so much its own motivation that it blows your mind. But making love the five hundredth time? My first true poem was written with tears pouring down my face. Then the tears turned to sweat.

DM: You say you have begun writing a new sequence. Do you have a sense of the work's direction?

WE: Actually, I write out of the crises in my life. For

Virgo, this is the permanent condition, since it is the sign of crisis. We see this in Lawrence, a true Virgo, the condition of the sensibility in permanent crisis with itself, from which his art could not deliver him, and which burned him up. But my sensibility is not all exacerbated, and my religion came in my life at a time when the crisis became absolute, and gave me comfort. Nevertheless, the contour of crisis constitutes the contour of formality in what I do. The only sense of direction is the sense of crisis engaged.

However, I simply wasn't prepared for this terminal break with the Order. As I say, leaving was more of an upheaval than a decision. Now that I have truly begun again, I rejoice. Because I see how right it is. I don't mean in the moral sense. I only mean I am delivered from having to elaborate what no longer required elaboration.

For in beginning again, right or wrong, you are restored to fundamentals. Nature, love, the touch of woman, Susanna. And something never before in my life, or in my poetry: the child. Little Jude makes it all new.

Fall, 1969

Lawrence Ferlinghetti

1

LF: I have nothing to say. I haven't got my crystal spectacles on.

DM: You just published a book? (*Tyrannus Nix*)

LF: I don't have anything to say in relation to all these other poets. I don't feel myself to be part of any scene now. I never went in for the regional point of view. I don't know anything about anything! That's the way I feel. I am living in Big Sur a lot of the time and I really don't have much to do with what is going on now.

DM: Is this a transitional period for you?

LF: Definitely. When isn't it? In the summer I'm a Nudist Anarchist; in the winter I'm a Buddhist Socialist.

DM: Your new book of poems . . . can we consider that to be a statement of your concern?

LF: It is the old political bullshit. Politics is a drag, but every once in a while you get dragged into it and have to sound off. But it is not my idea of an ideal kind of poetry.

JS: It is not your constant concern . . .?

LF: No. I keep getting dragged into that bag and I get classified as a political poet. I had another book that came out this year called *The Secret Meaning of Things,* which is generally not political at all.

JS: You have written a poem now about every president since Eisenhower . . .

LF: That is just what Snyder said.

JS: It seems you have an overwhelming historical concern . . .

LF: No, I haven't. I wrote a poem about Eisenhower and I wrote this one about Nixon. It seems to me there were very few presidents in between. I wrote about Fidel Castro in between. The last president of the U.S.A. was really Fidel Castro. He ran things from down there in Cuba even when Kennedy was president. Castro was acting and the U.S.A. was forced to react according to its already well-established guidelines for Christian behavior and, therefore, had to react strictly according to the American way of life which he threatened. Castro may still be president. Nixon is sort of a bush-league stand-in.

The Cuban Revolution was the Spanish Civil War of my generation. The thing that turned on the writers in the thirties was the Spanish Civil War. It would be interesting to pin down some of the other poets you have interviewed as to what their actual position is on Castro. I find a good many of the poets around are quite rightist, if not reactionary, and most of them are politically illiterate. Great Kerouac is not around anymore, so we won't go into him. But there's a Hemingway parallel there.

I recently received a list of award winners from the National Foundation of the Arts. Many poets and little presses in the country have received grants from them. This is government money in the form of grants from either the National Foundation of the Arts and Sciences or the Coordinating Council of Little Magazines and Small Presses.

Jean-Jacques Lebel and I had a running argument over the last six weeks while he was staying here. He considers himself a revolutionary, and he proposed that a young poet he met in Berkeley get a $1,000 grant from this foundation. There was a scout in town, Gus Blaisdell, from the University of New Mexico. He was looking for people to recommend for government grants. Jean-Jacques Lebel suggested Blaisdell recommend the young Berkeley poet. It happened that Blaisdell didn't dig this fellow's poetry. That wasn't my point.

My point was that it surprised me that someone who considered himself a full-blown revolutionary would be the first to accept government money. Even though I dig that using establishment money for antiestablishment ends *is* subversive—part of the cultural "rip-off." The Kayak Press in San Francisco, for instance, took $10,000 two years in a row. One of the editor's justifications was that he would sponsor a prize for the best poem on Che Guevara. The *prize* for the best poem on Che Guevara was $400, I believe. I have heard that the Kayak editor, George Hitchcock, was a radical in the thirties and it seems to me that this is sort of what happened to the whole old liberal movement in this country. The labor unions were bought off. They loaded the ships for Vietnam. From my point of view, which I admit is disputable, poets and little presses are also being bought off. Any one of them that took the money would say, "No, that's not true. We are free to do anything we want with the money." But it's logical that if you're a real Bad Boy the first year, you won't get the grant renewed. And then too—someone in another country—a radical in France or Germany— reads about your taking this money and they don't

see the rationalization and the various gradations of
your reasoning. All they see is the fact that you took
the U.S. government money. . . . I guess mine is the
"pure" purist position—though I hardly consider myself "pure"—

JS: Perhaps what happens today is that most poets
of David's generation and the younger poets of my
generation don't take the whole thing that seriously.
And free money is . . .

LF: Jean-Jacques's argument was that it depends on
what you use the money for. If you take the money to
live on, that is one thing. But if you take it to instigate a
plot to blow something up, or to throw sand in the
wheels of the machine, then it is justified. He said
this kid in Berkeley is interested in using money to
buy materials to hatch a big plot. . . . The kid doesn't
have time to work because he is working full-time on
the revolution. This Government money will save
him from having to get a job and he can work full-
time on blowing up the system. I have a note in
Tyrannus Nix that I would like to get on the
record, page 82. It is a note about a line called "The
poets and their sad likenesses":

*"Many American poets do in fact help the govern-
ment in sanctioning a status quo which is supported
by and supports WAR as a legal form of murder:
witness the number of avant garde poets and little
presses who have in recent years accepted U. S. grants
directly from the National Foundation of the Arts or
from its conduit, the Coordinating Council of Literary
Magazines and Little Presses, making it clear that
the avant garde in the arts is not necessarily to be
associated with the political left. See Marcuse's 're-
pressive tolerance,' that is, the policy of tolerance
and/or sponsorship as a self protection against violence; or as Susan Sontag recently put it, 'Divesting
unsettling or subversive ideas by ingesting them.' The
State, whether capitalist or Communist, has an enor-*

mous capacity to ingest its most dissident elements."
DM: In what sense does a poet help revolution, if at all . . . and what is the revolution?
LF: It depends on which revolution you are talking about. I mean, the first thing a poet has to do is to live that type of life which doesn't compromise himself. It seems to me that taking government grants and living on them is compromising himself before he even starts writing.
JS: I heard an answer to it while I was involved with the Unicorn Press and they were disputing the matter of taking government money. George Hitchcock presented a very realistic position for taking the money and using it in an almost anarchistic way. He stated that he wanted to be left alone and that this money would help insulate him against the system. He then brought up the point of hypocrisy in consumption. We live in America now and consume American goods and do, in fact, work and do our business in American cities. We are supporting the system in almost every way and to refuse free money seems almost silly. I mean, we are all buying goods that indirectly help support the war.
LF: You can't breathe, you can't live in a country, walk down its streets, use a car, and certainly not operate a business, or buy anything in a store, without having to cooperate against your will. The point is what you have a choice to do and what you don't have a choice to do. You do have the choice of deciding whether or not you are ingested by the state voluntarily and thus becoming a functioning part of it—nourishing it symbiotically, so to speak. The carrot and the stick—*Waiting for Godot* still—Pozzo with Lucky the artist on a string—The next time Nixon runs for office, for instance, he can say he sponsored or supported you. So vote for him, baby. Let's not spoil the Spoils System.

From another point of view: say you are running a

press . . . I was never offered a grant personally because I didn't apply for one. But I had some correspondence with Carolyn Kizer about people to recommend for these grants. I wasn't cooperating with her at all. I didn't wish to cooperate as the director of a press. It is doubly bad for a press to take government money. It is almost like a newspaper taking it.

JS: What about independent grants like the Guggenheim and the Ford Foundation?

LF: The radical would say that these large foundations are just as big murderers as the government is. Are they? I figure it is important to lead the kind of life where you don't have to take grants from any organization. You have to make it on your own without any help. At any point you can tell them to go fuck themselves. And not only can but do tell them. The real problem is to decide who's "them." . . . Well, you can say or print anything you want, according to the government foundations. The director of the program is obviously sincere in saying that there are no strings attached to the money. Grants are renewable the second year. Suppose during the first year you publish something that is really offensive politically, or offensive to the sensibilities of those in Washington who hold the purse strings? If you say "Fuck you, Agnew" will you get your grant renewed the second year? Maybe yes.

Here is a part of Carolyn Kizer's reply to me . . . "I see no reason why the government shouldn't subsidize attacks on itself. After all, this endowment gave $10,000 to Grace Paley whose activities in various Viet Nam and Peace movements are well known, and another $10,000 to Robert Duncan, who is not exactly friendly to our foreign policy. Why should you be? And what does that have to do with creative art? No, the attack will come, and is coming, from Congress. One congressman has just sent for all the books written by people to whom we have given grants thus far. And it will continue when our anthologies from the best writings from literary magazines appears, because every literary magazine in the country has been asked to take part in this program. I am sorry that you don't wish to accept any aid from an organization that bears the Great Seal on its letterhead. I myself don't feel that this is the same as refusing an invitation to the White House. Neither does Lowell, for that matter, with whom I am in frequent consultation . . ."

Obviously, the government and congressmen scrutinize the presses who are given money, as she says they are doing in this letter.

Here she says, "Perhaps a similar plan would be feasible for independent small presses. Perhaps I should point out to you that some care and judgment involving considerations not wholly aesthetic will be imperative, particularly in the early stages of such a program. Work chosen for partial Federal subsidy will be subject to the closest scrutiny by persons anxious to attack the Federal Arts Program. Part of the responsibility for this program lies in the development of receptive audiences for the best works of art produced by society—irrespective of how they may offend taboos of specific groups. My own feeling is that shock treatment isn't suitable under such circumstances, but rather a slow and laborious process of increasing exposure to art in all its forms—not the least of which is books beautifully composed and beautifully produced."

Shock treatment isn't in order . . . but rather a slow easy careful development. That's it exactly—from a revolutionary viewpoint today, it *is* time when shock treatment is necessary! It sounds like the Old South when they say, "We can't have any fast changes . . . things have to develop slowly . . . you can't rush the desegregation . . ." and so forth. The blacks were fed up with that and started blowing things up. White radicals feel it is definitely time for shock treatment these days. And it seems to me that most of the poets, especially in San Francisco, are on the whole very quiet. They are certainly not engaging in any shock treatment. Neither for legalizing psychedelics, or preventing ecocatastrophe or preventing world war.

DM: There have been probably more benefit poetry readings this last year than there have ever been. One a week almost. All concerns: ecological concerns, against the war, draft benefits, People's Park . . . it seems like it has been easy to amass large groups of poets to read for nearly any benefit and cause . . .

LF: Who is reading books of poetry these days? The rock generation certainly isn't . . . say under the age of twenty-five. What books are they reading! If you went to the Fillmore and took a poll on how many people have read even Ginsberg, you would probably get about 5 percent. They just aren't reading books, it seems. The whole revolution of the sixties was psychedelic and visual and oral: the poster trip and the rock trip . . . the book wasn't it. Maybe now it is *Zap Comics*. The amount of *Zap Comics* we sell at the bookstore is enormous. The average dude who comes in and buys tickets to the Fillmore buys *Zap Comics*. They articulate his "community" for him. They articulate his "counterculture"—and City Lights bookstore just got busted for selling *Zap*—we haven't been "ingested" yet.

JS: What would he buy ten years ago if he came in?

LF: Literature . . . Ginsberg. . . .

JS: I am under twenty-five, I dig rock music, but I and a circle of friends that is relatively large have always been reading, hanging around bookstores . . .

LF: I was thinking of a group younger than you. Maybe it is splitting hairs about how young . . .

JS: I think a great deal of the movement is concerned with books . . .

LF: Reading books isn't the greatest thing in the world, maybe. We overdid it in my generation. Maybe it's not so all-important to be literate. This new book of mine that New Directions put out, *Tyrannus Nix,* they printed a lot of copies, but what is it going to change? It is not going to change anything, it seems to me. A good rock concert may change people's consciousness faster. That was the argument before Altamont, anyway.

JS: Let's trace one book. What about *Howl?* (Those early City Lights books meant a lot to people in my high school.) Let's bring it down to the nitty-gritty. . . . Is *Howl* selling more than it did five or ten years ago?

LF: Well, yes. It is selling more than it sold ten years ago and more than it sold five years ago, but this year the books on the list that sold most were the books by Brautigan. Brautigan's books outsold Ginsberg's, which is quite a surprise. Brautigan got identified with the hippie generation, though he was around long before hippies. He was around in the beat days, and the beat nights—

There were a few new young poets in the Haight-Ashbury, but none of them ever got well known. It's as if you had to have a guitar to make it. Ginsberg, McClure, Snyder, these were all holdovers, bridge figures from the fifties. Not many others made that bridge. . . . And how did these poets from the fifties bridge the gap? Some used some kind of musical instrument to back up their voices. Like Ginsberg using finger cymbals and then the harmonium . . . and Michael McClure using the autoharp, and I use an autoharp. These were all attempts to bridge this gap. The single unaccompanied voice couldn't stand up to a rock group. I mean, it's murder to come on stage after a good rock group as a single unaccompanied voice. I did this down in Santa Barbara. They had a benefit last spring for Resist, part of Robert Bly's

antiwar tour, and Rexroth was master of ceremonies.
. . . I didn't get on until 1:00 A.M. I was part of an
enormously long variety show program, and I had to
follow Mad River. That was really murder. I did one
long poem with a taped raga backing up my voice
(*Assassination Raga*).

I have been doing more with the autoharp lately.
In fact I have chanted some with Daniel Moore's
Floating Lotus Magic Opera. Daniel's trip is a very
definite part of revolution today. He pulls a lot of
separate things together.

JS: He is writing only for that now. He doesn't write
any more poetry.

LF: The libretto is his poetry. I mean it is very much
like the poetry he published in *Dawn Visions*. Daniel
Moore is really a musical and dramatic genius. Like
you have been through the Living Theater and you
have been through Artaud, and here comes Daniel
Moore out of all of that with a ceremonial ritual
drama. Daniel's solution to the single voice. He started
out with the single voice and then got the whole
Tibetan opera backing up his voice. One of the few
poets who can make it on his own voice is Ginsberg.

After the blast of the rock scene . . . in '65 and '66
. . . the San Francisco poets have been singularly
silent. There have been a lot of poetry readings but—
for instance—the big reading we had at Norse Auditorium a couple of years ago . . . you know, an awful
lot of awful poetry went down that night. Along with
some great stuff.

2

LF: There is a lot of talk about ecology and yet they will have five thousand people at Big Sur Hot Springs completely fouling up the landscape to attend an ecology seminar. Not to mention Altamont. There is really going to be an enormous ecological catastrophe, or ecocatastrophe, within the next ten years, unless something really drastic is done. Capitalism is an outrageously *extravagant* form of existence which is leading to an enormous ecological debacle unless it is completely changed.

Theodore Roszak in *The Making of a Counter-Culture* makes a point that the young radicals are picking on capitalism when they could just as well pick on technocracy in a Communist country. It seems obvious to me that capitalism has got to go. The world ecologically cannot afford capitalism anymore. It's absolutely absurd. An unplanned economy, a laissez-faire economy, or a semi laissez-faire economy, any kind of incentive capitalism, private incentive capitalism, these are luxuries the earth cannot stand anymore. The resources won't stand it. The pollution of the atmosphere won't stand it.

There has to be absolute population control on a worldwide basis. Not euthanasia, not compulsory killing of old people. . . . We will have to have worldwide contraception beginning at age twelve. People are going to have to have permission to have children. This is going to be an absolute necessity. We are going to have to do away with these medieval nationalistic forms of government and have a form of central planning. The whole world has got to be run by a huge supranational nonpolitical central planning agency.

It's got to be a form of humanitarian socialism: not authoritarian, but a nontotalitarian socialism. I'd like to think it could be a kind of Buddhist socialism. A planned Socialist economy is the only way we can avoid the absolute devastation of earth . . . the absolute pollution of earth. It has got to happen. I mean, it is really coming up to the way it is laid out in *2001: A Space Odyssey,* where all directions are coming from a central control somewhere. It's a very pessimistic point of view, but some sort of totalitarian supranational state seems unavoidable. I think it is practically impossible to avoid this. This is the last thing anyone wants, but it seems inevitable—whether by cataclysmic war which will end things up, with one strong central force in control, or by just plain ecocatastrophe. Capitalism just lays waste to too many resources. And the population jump that is going on now . . . "One half of the people that ever lived are still alive." Think that one over.

I had a poem called *After the Cries of the Birds Have Stopped*—it saw the world of the future where all that was left were roving bands of mystics . . . like those that we call mutants today would be the only ones left. Roving bands of long-haired mystics . . . the whole materialistic ideal of Western man in his business suit would go down the tube—

A lot of people think that practically any oriental religion has more to say and has more answers today than Christianity does . . . especially for the youth in this country. It's not that they give an optimistic view of the world or of the future, it's just that they are more realistic. Who can imagine going to a Christian church these days? There are a few exceptions, like the things that have been going on at some far-out churches which are engaging the young on their own terms . . . like the Glide Memorial, or the Free Church in Berkeley . . . that's where the Ho Chi Minh funeral parade ended up, at the Free Church in Berkeley . . .

JS: It is interesting that both of those churches you mentioned are in an Episcopalian framework. The church that most of us looked to a few years ago was the Unitarian one.

LF: The new Unitarian center in San Francisco . . . the architecture inside is like a Japanese building or a building somewhere in the Far East. It is a beautiful center and when Baba Ram Das (Richard Alpert) came back from India, that is where he spoke. He and other Jewish Buddhists, "Hindu Cantors," or rabbinic saddhus—

3

LF: I am surprised to find that quite a few poets in San Francisco keep guns. I heard that Gary Snyder, Lew Welch, and James Koller held target practice now and then. I wrote Snyder about it and said I felt it was a sellout of his own values to keep guns. He wrote back and said, well, he grew up in the Northwest where things were different from where I grew up in New York City. In the great Northwest, people had guns like household utensils, and it was just an ordinary object that everyone had for survival purposes. He stated his position, which I recognize, but it still didn't alter the basic argument, as far as I was concerned. If you keep guns then ultimately they are going to be used for the function they were built for. As long as there are guns, they will speak, telescopically. It looks like I'm stuck with the purist position again.

I met a wandering Japanese mystic here in the summer, Nanao Sasaki. He is a friend of Gary's. He is the one that founded that ashram on Suwanose Island. In fact he is the one that told me about Gary's having the gun. After I wrote this letter to Gary, Nanao said to me: "I'm going to add a P.S.: We do not *have* to survive."

I think there are an awful lot of misguided poets in the West, in SF. . . . I am not thinking of Gary Snyder now . . . there are plenty of other poets that believe in violence. From this you could explore violence on the left, or violence among radicals who consider themselves on the left. I think this is one reason that *Ramparts* magazine finds itself on the rocks. *Ramparts* is a good example of the radical left which supported black power right down the line. . . . Eldridge Cleaver is one of its editors, which is good, because Eldridge Cleaver has about twice as much brains as all the other black radicals that I know. What I meant was, the radical left turns out to have been supporting large elements of the radical right. The most violent elements in the Black Panthers or in the black power movement are not strictly to be identified with Eldridge Cleaver. Naturally, I think Cleaver is great because he seems at least to realize the blacks don't have a monopoly on revolution these days—

"Right on" has become the motto of black power,

shouted by many white radicals who never gave support to the word "right" before—there are all kinds of rightist elements at work in radical circles these days, white and black. For instance, when you say if someone doesn't agree with you, you are going to use force on him, we are going to beat him up, we are going to pull out guns if you don't agree with us— that's also fascist. The assumption of adopting the ideas of Che Guevara, or the principles of guerrilla warfare, as something workable in this country, is absurd, because this is a completely different setup with an entrenched government so powerful it couldn't possibly be overturned by any band of guerrillas or revolutionaries blowing up power plants. Guerrilla theory is based on the assumption that in the early stages of insurrection, the mass of the citizenry is going to rise up and support the guerrillas— and this just won't happen in the U.S.A. where the middle class is so well fed. Not until there is another great depression could it happen.

I took the plane from here to LA on the Friday afternoon Commuter Special. You are up there at 35,000 feet, sitting next to these executives. The one next to me had a plastic button that said, such and such a name, General Manager, Fairchild. These men ride along up there at 35,000 feet and they really are the Roman emperors of the world. They have got this enormous technocracy which they control: the military-industrial complex. It's not just a myth. They are actually ruling the whole earth, and it is so powerful that there is no possibility of this kind of entrenched establishment being overturned by any band of revolutionaries.

As, for instance, even in France it was possible for a student revolution to actually make the government fall, for the whole government to topple, and a new form of government to take its place.

DM: There are those who would say that the student

revolution, or the student-based anti-Vietnam movement, fought for in this country during the last five
years, caused Johnson to resign.

LF: I think that's true. People are always saying:
What good does it do to march in peace parades? The
snowballing peace movement, centered in peace
parades in those days, actually did cause Johnson
to decide not to run again. I mean, it seems obvious.

JS: Well, that would seem to be an effective ploy
against the military-industrial complex.

LF: But that's as far as it can go. It can't overthrow
the government itself and, as I said the other day,
the only way it can happen in this country is if there
is a great economic depression again, like in the
thirties. I think that will happen. Eventually there is
going to be another great boom and bust and then
we will have economic conditions where it will be
possible to have a real overthrow of the government.
That great depression might very well arrive before
this is printed—

Nationalism is a medieval form of government. The
whole argument during the American Civil War was
that the states wouldn't give up any of their states'
rights until the federal government could work. Now
nations still refuse to give up any sovereignty, or
states' rights, in the UN. They refuse to give up their
vetoes. And the U.S.A. is the first to refuse to give
any of its states' rights. You will have a civil war on a
world level so long as these countries won't give up
their stupid nationalistic forms. It will be an absolute
catastrophe unless they do.

Maybe everyone is getting hysterical on the subject
of ecology these days. But it seems to me that things
are moving very fast. Every day in the papers there
is another ecological disaster. Today there was a story
about "strange foreign birds" landing here and there.
Or, the day before, there was a "strange epidemic that
killed all the fish in the Berkeley estuary."

DM: These things have been going on for a long time. The results via the media seem to be more interesting to the public than the process itself.

LF: Someone said that the danger is people may well become bored with the word "ecology" before they really comprehend what it means. If we are fortunate, there will be a political revolution in this country which will allow a new ecological control of the world (which is a very doubtful possibility). Suppose you did arrive at a point where a planned economy was instituted? Then you could get down to what would happen to the individual. Is he going to be a mystic, or what is he going to do? Then the individual is free again to write poetry.

JS: Would you try to institute a government more concerned with distribution of goods, more concerned with planning, with making sure that somebody is not building too many tract homes . . . ?

LF: Right. That is why there needs to be an overall central planning.

JS: Sure, and that kind of central planning is for distribution of goods . . .

LF: Of course, this is what the Socialist countries are trying to do. This is what it was all about.

DM: You start off working theoretically with equal distribution of goods and all of a sudden, like in a matter of years, it winds up the same thing: somebody, a small nucleus of power, essentially more concerned with power than anything else—What is this peculiar continuity that takes place in revolution? Man reaches the point of overthrowing a so-called tyrannical government and, in turn, winds up propagating the same thing.

LF: Man is by nature predatory. It's too bad we can't all be just "predators of sweetness and light."

4

DM: One of the general questions we like to ask is, when do you recall your first responses to poetry, your first connection with it . . .?

LF: Up to now, if I had some biographical question to answer, I would always make something up.

Who's Who sent a questionnaire form and for several years I wrote "Fuck you!" on the *Who's Who* questionnaire, and sent it back to them. But they are very persistent people and they keep writing and they keep saying, "If you don't answer this, we will publish something about you which may not be correct—so you may as well correct this"—so you get involved correcting a column of type that they have written about you that they have scrounged from other. sources. I make up a lot of things.

Was I probably born in 1919 or 1920 in either Paris or New York? Some days it's hard to tell. I really don't see the reason for giving a straight answer. For one thing, I enjoy putting on *Who's Who.* I have done this with a lot of different interviewers, since it is valid for a poet who considers himself a semi-surrealist poet.

If you are going to write in one manner and someone comes to you with some straight questions—why should you give them a straight answer?

For instance, there was a very serious French professor from the Sorbonne who did a long serious book on American poets, and he interviewed me on tape. He asked me what my thesis was at the Sorbonne—what my doctor's thesis was there. I told him that it was the history of the pissoir in French literature. The interview was in French. And he wrote it all down and it came out in the book that my doctoral thesis at the Sorbonne was called *The History of the Pissoir in French Literature.* He is really pissed now. He found out. They'll have to change the index cards in the Sorbonne where the damn thing is filed. Maybe the place will be burnt down in the next revolution. That would help.

The way I happened to get into surrealism just now is that I've been talking to Philip Lamantia, who has just come back into town. It's really kind of exciting. He has a place in North Beach, a block from City Lights. He is working with Steve Schwartz who has started a surrealist magazine, *Anti-Narcissus.* Then there is Nanos Valaoritis, who is an exile Greek poet-professor at State College. He is more or less identified with French surrealism. He edited a magazine in Greece which was a surrealist magazine. I am going to publish a book of their surrealist texts, I think. The whole thing comes together after all these years. We talk and think about some word better than surrealism. At a time when daily reality far exceeds "literary" surrealism, there really isn't any better term. I mean, maybe there is, but no one has thought of it yet. Superrealism? Hyperrealism? Unrealism?

Philip and I have had some funny surrealistic experiences since he has returned here. We wrote a poem about one one day. I wrote a surrealist poem about the surrealist enigma of Ho Chi Minh's funeral and how a girl we met in North Beach, whom we called Nadja, opened the door of her womb to Philip Lamantia, and inside was a light bulb. Turn her on—

Anyway, I have been telling Philip that I don't see

why he doesn't consider me a surrealist, too. He says I am just writing fake surrealist poems. Well, he didn't say "fake surrealist poems," but I had the feeling he thought I was doctoring up my spontaneous visions and putting "thought" in it—making it no longer a pure surrealistic product. In fact, I *was* doctoring them up. Hyping them up, might be more accurate.

DM: It would be interesting to know your early sources, your early teachers . . .

LF: The surrealist poets were some of my earliest sources. Especially poets like Apollinaire, who was not really a surrealist. He was more or less the con man of the movement, but I think I learned more from him than others.

JS: You chose to go to France to school?

LF: My mother was French. I was in France with her when I was a kid. . . . That's not true. [*Laughter*.] . . . Strike that. I was in France with one of my relatives, one of my French relatives . . . you can never tell whether these statements are true or not . . . I was kidnapped by . . . now this is absolutely true [*Laughter*.] . . . I was kidnapped by a man, a French cousin of my mother's, who took me to France in swaddling clothes and didn't bring me back to the U.S.A. until I was about six or seven years old.

So later I had some memory of speaking French, and it wasn't too hard to get back to it. It was a natural thing to go back to.

I went to Columbia and got an M.A. but the idea of getting a Ph.D. at Columbia was so forbidding . . . the whole discipline and regime you had to go through to get an American Ph.D. . . . yet I wanted to use the GI Bill as much as I could. . . . So I went to Paris on it.

The whole thing about a doctorate at the University of Paris was that you were a free man. You just had to report to the director of your thesis like once every half year. You could spend decades working on your thesis—some eternal students did just that—one on Rimbaud—they didn't care whether you ever came back. I remember going to the "soutenance"—the public defense of your thesis. It's like the orals they have in this country, but it is in one of those big renaissance lecture halls they have at the Sorbonne, and is open to the public. You have a jury of professors up on the stage. You sit with your back to the audience and the professors are up there in their robes and they work your thesis over and ask you questions about it, in classical French, and you're supposed to reply in classical French. I guess that was one of the things French students revolted against about two years ago. I must say I made some classic mistakes. I defended translation mistakes by saying that a translation is like a woman—when she is faithful she is not beautiful—when she is beautiful she isn't faithful—

I was free, and this was ideal for someone who wanted to find time and bread to be a writer. To get my monthly GI check, all I had to do was sign a book once a month at the Sorbonne. I got five full years out of the GI Bill that way. And never went to class.

JS: What was your thesis eventually on?

DM: The pissoir?

LF: What thesis? [*Laughter.*] This is absurd. In fact . . . it was on modern poetry: the *city* in modern poetry, in French and English poetry. In English there are things like Hart Crane's *Bridge* and Eliot's *Waste Land.* All this fits into city poetry. Things like Francis Thompson's *City of Dreadful Night.* And in French, long poems like Verhaeren's' *Tentacular City*—

DM: When was this?

LF: It could have been after the Second World War, centuries ago.

I didn't know any literary people at all when I was living in France in those days, and I didn't know any Americans who were there writing. Rexroth later told me: "Now I remember I met you in Paris, and you knew so-and-so and so-and-so . . . I'm sure I knew you . . ." But I didn't know any of the people he says I met. Or it was another me. The first I heard of Rexroth was when I read his introduction to the *Selected Poems of D. H. Lawrence*—he really turned me onto Lawrence. I was living with a French family over in the workers' part of town, near Père Lachaise cemetery, on Place Voltaire. I lived with the family of an old Communist. An old man who looked like Beethoven and who was a music professor, a classical music teacher. I went to the Sorbonne once a month to sign this book and otherwise I didn't have anything to do with any literary scene.

I got a place of my own in Montparnasse which cost me about twenty-six dollars a year. It was a cellar with two rooms and a little tiny air-shaft kitchen with a sink hollowed out of solid stone, which must have been there since the Middle Ages, and a front room that had a French window on a courtyard. That was the only window in the two rooms. The middle room had no windows at all. It was very damp in there. And it was dark. There was only light from this front window.

I got the place by sneaking in one night. It was absolutely impossible to find any apartments in Paris. Even today you have to buy the key and it costs an enormous amount.

I met a plumber in a bar and he was tubercular and his wife and children were tubercular. He had three children and they were all living in this dank two-room apartment and it was very damp and the kids were coughing and they were all sick—and he owed everyone in the neighborhood. We agreed that I would pay up all his debts in the neighborhood so he could leave, and he would move me in at night, and when the concierge came the next day, I would tell her that I was a friend of his and that he was away in the country. So the whole thing cost me a hundred dollars to pay off all his debts. It went on like that for three years. I had this place and kept telling the concierge that he was coming back. Maybe me and the concierge and the plumber were the original models for *Waiting for Godot.* Of course the plumber never came back, and I finally sold the place the same way. Moved out in the middle of the night. That was the place where I wrote *Her.* It wasn't a novel, it wasn't supposed to be a novel. It was a surrealist notebook that I kept, a Black Book. It is a book which New Directions calls a novel. They have to call it something. But it never got any reviews in this country. It came out in 1958 or 1959, right after *Coney Island of the Mind,* although I had written the first version of it in 1949 or '50. This book has never gotten any reviews in this country. I got some in France when it came out in French because it fits into the French tradition of the novel. Like you can fit it in the Robbe-Grillet and Breton's *Nadja.*

Nadja was one of the books I stole from them. I also stole from Djuna Barnes's *Nightwood.* It's full of all kinds of stuff I stole from *Nightwood*—which I always thought was one of the great American expatriate novels. Really great prose. I once told Djuna Barnes that I thought her prose was man's prose, and she said that was the greatest compliment I could have paid her.

The speeches of Dr. Matthew O'Connor are absolutely great prose. They find him in bed dressed as a woman, and he talks of the Night. Watchman, what of the Night. He lays it out. . . .

In this country there is no tradition for a novel like *Her.* The critics don't know what to do with it; they don't have anywhere to place it. It doesn't fit in any-where. The closest thing I can think of is the work of Anaïs Nin—Virginia Woolf under water—though what she is saying and what she is preoccupied with is completely different. In fact she wrote a book about the novel *The Novel of The Future* in which she listed *Her*. That is the only reference I have ever seen to *Her* in this country.

LF: Why is it that there has never been anyone really following *Finnegans Wake* in this country? What happened after that was a complete disintegration of the language and a dissociation of imagery which went into "cutups." This is the same surrealist dislo-cation of imagery which Bill Burroughs arrived at through the physical cutting up of texts. The French and Italian surrealists did cutups and collages many years before. Of course, what was new in Burroughs was what he did with it. In him, you have an artificial dislocation of imagery, which is one direction writing could go after *Finnegans Wake*. Joyce had done that as far as one could possibly do it, with his enormous brain, and his superlinguistic genius. The cutup tech-nique produces the same dissociation of imagery, the same dislocation of imagery, only it is arrived at by mechanical means. In Burroughs' case it didn't come out of the Joycean vision at all . . . it came out of the junkie vision. It was too hard on his own body to keep up the junkie vision. To arrive at a different type of reality dislocation, he cut up the words by cutting up the paper, which was easier on his own head and body. He put down drugs and picked up a pair of scissors. Anyone who can pick up a frying pan—

DM: Is that what you could call native American surrealism: a strange, violent reaction to media, cut-ting it up and throwing it up . . . a sort of fragment-ing . . . ?

LF: Yes. McLuhan said it all, I guess. And we end up with no Joyceans.

DM: I don't think so. What about Jack Hirschman?

LF: Like in his book *Jah?*

DM: Sure. That's like the American *Finnegans Wake*.

LF: Hirschman doesn't have the utter brilliance of language and articulation of Joyce. Yet Hirschman has his own . . .

DM: I think it is there and will be known.

LF: Henry Miller never did any experimentation with language in this sense.

DM: But don't you think that those early books of Miller could act as a valuable contribution to native American surrealism . . . ?

LF: *Air Conditioned Nightmare* . . .

DM: Yes, and the *Tropics* and *Black Spring*. He was able to combine the lesson of Europe with the great Buffalo Bill American simplicity. Mickey Mouse faces three hundred years of culture . . .

LF: You know, Miller was attracted to Kerouac at one point. He discovered Kerouac quite late, evidently. I remember when *Dharma Bums* came out. Jack was out here and he was going to go to Big Sur to stay in my cabin. That is when he wrote a book called *Big Sur*. His editors must have named it, because it had nothing to do with Big Sur. He never really got into the Sur at all, never got south of Bixby Canyon. Miller was turned on to the *Dharma Bums*. They were talking to each other on the phone. Jack was here in City Lights and Miller was in Big Sur. They were going to meet for dinner at Ephraim Donner's house in Carmel Highlands. Miller went to Donner's and Jack was drinking in town here. The afternoon kept getting later and later. Kerouac kept saying, "We'll get there, we'll leave soon . . ." It got later and later and Jack kept telling them on the phone, "We're leaving now. We'll be there in three hours . . . two-and-a-half hours, we'll make it in two . . . Cassady will drive me

. . . we'll be there in no time. See you at seven." At seven Kerouac is still in town drinking. Eight o'clock. Nine o'clock . . . Miller is sitting, waiting. Kerouac never got there. And I don't think they ever did meet. That was the end of it.

Dharma Bums had all the elements that would appeal to Miller. The on-the-road trip, the air-conditioned nightmare, the mountaintops, and that freedom . . . the whole idea of dharma bums.

I haven't seen Kerouac in a long time . . . but I imagine that Jack is probably sitting in front of his TV set, wearing a baseball cap, with a bottle of Skid Row tokay, watching the ball game on TV in central Florida. Something seemed to die in him early in the 1950s—the Hemingway parallel again. Killing himself. Yet, by age forty-seven, he's written more and better than the Great Hunter . . .

5

LF: The French intellectual is something that I put down lately. The whole French civilization has led to their having become very effete. Even many of the ones involved in the May revolution last year. The difference between the young radical out here on the West Coast and the French intellectual is enormous. The American can do things himself with his hands . . . he is into the whole Survival thing. There's no such thing as the *Whole Earth Catalog* in France.

Of course, there are utopian communes there, but you have no such thing as groups that are doing everything themselves, making everything themselves, like leather, clothes, books, tools, and so on . . .

The intellectual in Europe is like the intellectual in South America, Latin America. He doesn't wash dishes, for instance. Still a woman's place to do all that crap. The intellectual in Latin America (this isn't so in France) may talk very revolutionary ideas, but he is usually very well dressed in a white shirt, necktie, and even cuff links. When Ginsberg and I went to South America in 1959 this surprised me. We met poets and writers and intellectuals and professors from all the South American countries at this conference in Concepción. Including a lot of Communists. And practically everyone was meticulously dressed. They didn't have drip-dry shirts in those days either. In other words, there was a housekeeper, a *criada* back home, ironing those shirts and doing the laundry. No one questioned this, in public at least . . .

The second big difference I found was there were no mystic trips going on in France. Naturally, there are older mystics and there have always been writers. René Daumal for instance *Mount Analogue* but in the young kids, the revolutionary-age groups, there's little mysticism . . . nothing like the Hare Krishna Society or Zen or Gurdjieff. The kids who are turned on to Gurdjieff in America, however, don't realize the European background for the movement. Claude Pelieu is a French poet and translator living in the States, and he enlightened me on the history of Gurdjieff in Europe. I don't know whether this is all true, but it seems that Gurdjieff was a White Russian refugee from the Revolution. He left Russia in 1917 or so, and made quite a few counterrevolutionary statements at that time. Then he traveled to the Near East and had some contact with the Sufis. It's in his books *Conversations with Remarkable Men.*

During the Second World War, according to Pelieu, Gurdjieff was living in the suburbs of Paris and received Hitler and several of Hitler's main henchmen. In London and Paris Gurdjieff's followers were rich dilettantes. Rich old ladies and members of the upper leisure class.

They have a big hang-up on money in the Gurdjieff groups. You have to pay quite a lot of bread to attend, in some groups at least. Over here, the kids don't realize the possibly neofascist tendencies. Of course, Gurdjieff shouldn't be held responsible for what various followers have done with his ideas in America.

I mentioned before the neofascist tendencies among radicals. And it is in things like scientology, which is very full of neofascist ideas. I would class them all together as a sort of psychic authoritarianism.

JS: A friend of mine did a study at UBC. His doctoral thesis was on the fascist approach of youth today and how it is like the German youth of the late twenties and early thirties. Then the kids about my age were going to the woods and reading Hermann Hesse. They were carrying backpacks and hitchhiking all over the country. Women were hitchhiking publicly, singly. My friend firmly believed that the movement today is turning toward a kind of neofascism, toward a kind of psychic or intellectual fascism. Very strange. You can probably document it. Especially in Berkeley now. If you are not a member of the team, you are an enemy. The only escape is to claim that you are a visionary incompetent. That's the only way I make it. I go and say that I am not going to march on your line, and I am not a black power advocate, etc., etc., because I have something working in my mind that makes it impossible for me to participate in your physical revolution. They all allow me, but they won't allow another person who is just a good middle-class liberal, just simpatico. Very strange. But they will allow visionary incompetents. In fact they encourage them. They figure these people to be as harmless as any.

6

LF: I came to SF in December of 1950. Rexroth was the center of the scene. Robert Duncan was here. There was also a scene around Duncan. Rexroth used to have Friday night open houses for all the poets who would go sit at his feet. I was very timid when I was living in France and I would never dream of looking up a "literary figure." When Allen goes to France, he looks up everybody. He looked up Michaux or Céline . . . I would never think of going out and meeting these people on my own.

When I came to SF I heard about Rexroth. I heard about him through Holly Bye who was a friend of Kenneth Patchen's. Holly Bye was married to a printer named David Ruff and they had a printing press. I met Patchen through Holly Bye.

The Patchens were living in North Beach. Patchen moved from the East Coast in about 1955, I think. I was living in an attic in Pacific Heights. I met Holly because she had gone to Swarthmore with Kirby, my wife. They were at Swarthmore together and so she was the only person we knew here . . . the first person who had anything to do with any literary scene, and I think they took me over to Rexroth's house for the first time in about 1953. I was completely tongue-tied. I mean, he was a great man. I wasn't about to say anything! I went back for years before I even opened my mouth. I mean, even when he moved over to Scott Street, I was still the same way. I never said anything over there. I was too bashful to speak up. It was only in the late 1950s that I felt I could carry on a discussion with him.

DM: Was Kenneth Patchen sick when you first met him?

LF: He walked with a cane even then, but he was able to get around. He walked and shopped around North Beach. Shopping bag and cane. The Patchens lived on Green Street in North Beach and he would come to the bookstore a lot. Except once. After we started publishing books, around 1955, it was Patchen's idea to have an autograph party for his book (*Poems of Humor and Protest*). We announced it and a crowd came, but he never showed up. That was the first and last time I ever gave an autograph party! His wife Miriam called up and said Patchen was feeling too bad to come.

Then his back got worse and worse. They moved to Palo Alto to be near the hospital and they are still down there. It is in a sort of cul-de-sac off the freeway. And he just can't get out. He's just too sick. Painkillers all the time. It's a fucking tragedy. One of the great original American voices. And Stanford University has—so far as I know—never even recognized his presence. They should at least give him an honorary title of poet-in-residence. Even if they can't find a cent for him. It's disgraceful. Well, he doesn't need Stanford! I talked to him on the phone this week, for the first time in about a year. He said he had been a prisoner of his room for ten years. He sounds awful on the phone, obviously in pain . . .

DM: Does the future look any brighter for him?

LF: No. He's had so many operations on his back. The Patchens once sued the doctors for malpractice, which was a very bad thing to do, because the case was thrown out of court and the real result was that no doctor would take his case. He would come up here and sit in the lobby of the hospital and no doctor would touch him. He's been wanting to move away from this area, to go somewhere where he isn't black-balled by the medical profession.

The Patchens have investigated Florida and places like Tucson where the climate is good, but he said on the phone last week: "There's one thing I can't tolerate still, and that is intolerance."

DM: When did you first start publishing City Lights books?

LF: We started the bookstore in June of 1953. There was Pete Martin, who was an instructor in sociology at State College, and he was also a film buff. Pete Martin put out a magazine which was sociologically oriented toward film. It was called *City Lights*, an early pop-culture publication. It had people like Pauline Kael writing in it, and Mickey Martin, and the Farbers . . .

I don't know where I saw the magazine *City Lights*. There was a total of five or six issues and, for some reason, I sent them some of my translations of Jacques Prévert. I discovered North Beach around this time, about 1952. The Black Cat was the first place I ever went to and then the Iron Pot. I met Pete Martin around then. He said, "Oh, you sent me those Prévert translations!" He used them, and I think that was the first thing I ever got published.

The bookstore was started to pay the rent for the magazine at the same location, 261 Columbus. That little second floor was the magazine office. I didn't have anything to do with the magazine, but I started the bookstore downstairs with Pete Martin. The idea was that we would open it up a few hours a day. Pete Martin was full of great ideas. He now runs a bookstore in New York, called the New Yorker Bookstore. I've never been in it but I'm sure it's one of the most original around, knowing Pete—

In those days there were no pocket bookstores in the country. There weren't any pocket books except Penguins and the cheap ones you found in drugstores. And there was no place to buy them except in places like drugstores. It's pretty hard to imagine no paperback bookstores, but this was in 1953. So Pete Martin's idea was to have this place that had nothing but the best pocket books and to have all the political magazines, from left to right, which you couldn't get anywhere else. As soon as we opened the place, we couldn't get the door closed. Right from the beginning it was open until midnight, seven days a week, since 1953.

Pete Martin had so many ideas that he'd take off on something else before he finished the first thing. He split for New York after our first year. Got married or divorced and the bookstore just continued. We started publishing in 1955. Just poetry . . .

JS: The books were typically modeled after French books . . . ?

LF: The little ones, the Pocket Poets Series. The first ones we put out had a pasted-on label. I got this idea from Patchen's early edition of *An Astonished Eye Looks out of the Air,* which had a pasted-on label window around the middle of it, with the title on it. The first one was done by hand. David Ruff and Holly Bye and Kirby and myself and Mimi Orr pasted on covers and gathered it by hand, like any other little press. The first printing was a thousand copies. . . .

[The first publication of the Pocket Poets Series was *Pictures of the Gone World* by Ferlinghetti.]

Howl was the fourth book. The second was Rexroth's *30 Spanish Poems of Love and Exile,* and Patchen's *Poems of Humor and Protest* was the third book. And then came *Howl.* Now we are printing 20,000 at a crack on Ginsberg's books, on the reprints of all his books—*Planet News, Reality Sandwiches, Kaddish, Howl* . . . it's a lot of books of poetry. About once a year these books have to be reprinted. The first edition of "Howl" was only 1,500 copies.

We have over fifty books in print now. We were distributing a lot of other little presses up to this year, like Dave Hazelwood, Four Seasons, Don Allen, Coyote, to fill out our list. It was an interesting thing to do. One bookstore where other bookstores could order all these little press books. We put them all together in one catalog and sent it across the country to libraries and book dealers. But it got to be too big, too much work. This year I decided I'd just have to slough off the little presses and just do our own books. . . . We were hung up in the city doing the dirty work on getting the books around the country, while half of the small-press editors were out in their communes turned on. I was also put off by the little presses taking government money. Most of them were taking grants from the National Foundation of the Arts, and I disagreed with doing that, and I didn't want to be caught up in cooperating in this.

I don't take any bread out of it now. I live on my royalties from New Directions. I used to work at the store like forty hours a week. Shig is the one that has always put in thousands of hours a week. The store couldn't have existed without him. He is the one that has really held it together all these years.

I haven't worked regularly at the bookstore in five

or six years. In the fifties I worked there regularly and that is what I lived on. I used to draw about $300 a month at the most.

The bookstore really is unintentionally a nonprofit operation. Like in that old joke. For years the bookstore supported the publishing, now the publishing is better off than the bookstore. The bookstore keeps going but there are more and more books and there never is any cash left over after the fucking government gets paid! There are a lot of people living off it, though. We have six or eight people working. It's a good way to live, an interesting way to live—to say the least!

I have always believed in paying authors good royalties . . . as much as the New York publishers pay for paperback books. In fact, Allen Ginsberg gets more, because of the volume of his books. He gets more than paperback publishers normally pay. I don't know whether you would want to know how much royalties he got last year, but he got about $10,000 from City Lights. Which is a lot for a little press. The bottom dog on our list is Edward Dahlberg's *Bottom Dogs* so far as copies sold each year go.

DM: I guess you will be going on a reading tour now. . . .

LF: Yes. I will be. It would be ideal when I go on a college reading tour to have something to back up my voice with. This is not to say that the voice can't make it on its own. It can make it on its own in a traditional reading, in a room with a lot of graduate students sitting there, the traditional type of poetry reading with a lot of polite murmuring and polite applause . . . but when you get into a mass scene where you have an enormous audience, not only do you have to have poems that have a good deal of "public surface" and might be considered performance poems, but it takes a very exceptional voice to make it with an enormous audience. Allen Ginsberg is one of the few that makes it. He can be on the same program with a rock group because he has such a marvelously full voice. He could read the phone book and make it sound like a great poem.

For a person with a normal voice, like myself, it's great if you can use something like an autoharp. I can use an autoharp at home, but it is kind of cumbersome to carry around the country. . . . I can use it at home and turn on and get high chanting. But to do this at a big public reading . . . the idea is to come up with what you might call an American mantra.

One thing about the autoharp is that it is an indigenous American instrument. It's not like using the sitar or tamboura. And if you are using a guitar, you have to have a certain level of professional competence—unless you play it upside down in some cuckoo fashion and beat on it with a chopstick, or play it with your teeth, or something. Otherwise, I wouldn't get up on the stage with my guitar.

You can't take just any old poem and strum to it in the background. I am not talking about that. Nothing was worse than most of the poetry and jazz in the fifties. Most of it was awful. The poet ended up sounding like he was hawking fish from a street corner. All the musicians wanted to do was blow. Like, "Man, go ahead and read your poems but we gotta blow."

Krishnamurti was here last winter and he was at a party. I asked him what he thought of chanting Hare Krishna and he said, "Might as well chant Coca-Cola or Ave Maria." Kirby walked up and asked him for his autograph. And he refused. She really admired him. She had just finished reading one of his books and was very sincere about it. It was a faculty party after he'd given a lot of lectures in Berkeley. Mostly faculty people—everyone standing around in those cocktail dresses, suits; and he sort of away in a far end by himself. Kirby walks up with this book and pen and asks him to sign it. He would not sign it. He said: "Too much vanity." She felt really put down. It seemed to me that it is much more vain to refuse an autograph than to sign one.

I had a strange "conversation" with him, because he seemed very ill at ease at this party, like he didn't know whom to talk to. He didn't want to talk to all these people who looked like they were made of glass or plastic. He sort of looked like that, and I was the only guy in the room with a beard. This was before McClure and a whole contingent arrived. Anyway, Krishnamurti was standing around the punch bowl, but I couldn't get close enough to him to hear his voice. We were always about five feet apart. I would move up a little to hear his voice more clearly and he moved back, as if he were afraid, as if I were going to break his bones or something. He was a very fragile-looking man. The conversation went something like this—he said: "I don't eat meat." I said: "Big deal! Neither do a lot of my friends." He said, "But I have never *tasted* it." I said: "OK, you win." That was about the sum total of my exchange with Krishnamurti. Brilliant.

Speaking of influence . . . Blaise Cendrars's *On the Trans-Siberian* was written maybe sixty years ago. Well, I read it and took the train in 1967. I took the *Trans-Siberian* from Moscow across Siberia— seven days and six nights—on the basis of having read this poem. I got pneumonia and was in a seamen's hospital near Vladivostok in a town called Nakhodka, a workers' city. I damn near died! I could have died out there and no one would have known for months and months. It was on the Sea of Japan, and there were no communications whatsoever with the outside world. None with Japan, and the only communication was back to Moscow. I don't know how we got started on that, except . . . except the power of the poem. I mean, that shows what literature can do in the way of changing the world. (I damn near died, thanks to Blaise Cendrars.)

Spring, 1969

Lew Welch

1

LW: My mother was the daughter of a very famous surgeon in Phoenix. And her friends were President Hoover, Alan Campbell, the Goldwaters. The father and mother of Barry Goldwater killed my grandfather. Quite accidentally and sorrowfully. They would liked to have had it be any other way.

The story is this: You have a proud-born only daughter of a family, the Brownfields . . .

Six boys came from Ulster, Ireland, and it appeared that they had to come there because of some kind of political necessity. They were the Brownfields. They were peasants and their names came from peasant stock and somehow or other they had to come to America. And they did. And there were six of them, and they were all men, and the entire issue was my mother. Six men could have made a lot of children, but there was only one and that was my mother.

My mother married a man named Lew Welch and

155

he had one sister and she died when she was forty-four and he died when he was forty-seven. So you have in my life a thing very much like *Budden-brooks,* where you have the end of a very strong line. My sister will never have a child. I have never had a child from my loins. (I have and enjoy having two stepsons, but have none of my own.) My mother had myself and my sister and so it is over. The father is dead. The grandmothers on both sides are dead. There is nobody alive in my family except my mother, me, and my sister. And we are both barren.

My father was called Speed Welch because he was very fast in high-school football. In Redfield, Kansas, he was a very good fooball player and ran very fast. And how he met my mother, I have no idea. He really was very handsome. He looked like Tyrone Power and Cary Grant. I can show a photo to prove it. My mother naturally fell terribly in love with him. She really loved my father. It was a good love match. My mother had all the money, however. He didn't have a nickel.

He was the kind of guy that would play in the high sixties and low seventies in golf and knew everybody and didn't have a nickel unless it came from my mother. And she held on to her money. . . .

My grandfather looks exactly like me. It's spooky. You look at the goddamn photo and it's weird. My mother's father. A man named Robert Roy Brownfield. He was a man of great parts. He invented, among other things, the way of pulling out tonsils instead of cutting them. He was the first man to invent a decent machine to test hearing ability. He was a very fine surgeon. And he was also a sort of John Wayne–type cat. Seriously, he was an unbelievable man.

Robert Roy Brownfield never weighed more than 168 and was the heavyweight champ of the state of

Nebraska. He put himself through school and got to be a doctor, got his M.D. His father wanted him to be an engineer, and when he wanted to be a doctor, his father disowned him.

Bob Brownfield was a real gutty cat. He not only had to put himself through college, and did, but he became the amateur heavyweight champion of the state while doing it . . . *while* earning the money to get through school. A tough dude. I regret that I never met him.

He married a woman named Sims, Edith Sims, who came from a Pennsylvania Dutch family. They met in Nebraska and their only issue was my mother. His brothers all were without issue, except one, and that issue, whoever he was, disappeared. There is nobody left. Six strong boys came over from Ireland and six strong girls came out of Pennsylvania. And the whole thing produced only me and my sister.

My grandfather was probably the best surgeon in the West in 1920. Bob Brownfield knew more about the problems of cataracts than anyone. He operated on something like four thousand cataracts in a year and few had ever done forty in a whole lifetime. He would write papers about it and they would get published. Here it is 1910 and he was the first cat to want to buy an airplane.

You know what happened? My grandfather, Bob Brownfield, and his wife, Edie, and the Goldwaters, the parents of Barry, went to a country-club dance. And Bob had an operation to do the next morning and he didn't drink a drop. He said, "Please let me drive." And Mrs. Goldwater said, "I am all right, I'll drive." Bob Brownfield couldn't win the day and she drove. She made a mistake, rolled in a ditch, and he was dead at thirty-eight years old. His neck snapped.

And Mrs. Goldwater was so ashamed of herself. She was very lovely about it. The Goldwaters were very lovely. (Barry was my mother's schoolmate, about two years younger. He was a fat little Jewish boy that nobody liked. Spoiled rotten. The only Jew in Phoenix. The whole bit.) And Mrs. Goldwater would rather have died herself than to have killed Bob Brownfield. She loved him that much. He was a beautiful man. You could give him any musical instrument and he could learn it in a half hour, and would sing on it and make up the lyrics. I have whole books by Bob Brownfield. Short stories he wrote. They are terrible. But he was in there working. And he was a goddamn good doctor.

2

LW: My father, Lew Welch (I am a Junior), was the son of a very simple Kansas farmer and his wife. Real good, straight, go-to-church-every-Sunday American, Kansas people. I met them once when I was five. We spent a whole summer with them. And my grandfather had lost four fingers on his hand. He was a fuck-up. The Welches were fuck-ups. My grandfather was respected and loved by everybody in his county, but you wouldn't want to take him on a dangerous mission. That kind of thing.

You know what they finally did with Frank? (Frank Welch was my grandfather's name.) They finally made him a district judge because they respected him so much. They knew he could not make an immoral decision about anyone. He would be a great judge, even though he was stupid enough to cut all his fingers off on his right hand. And he always sold the land cheap when he should have sold it dear. And his cows always died. When he bought a bull it would always be sterile. Frank Welch had bad luck, they called it. But the community still loved this man so much they made him a judge and lived by his decisions. He lived the rest of his life, with his bum hand, as a judge. And no one ever pretended he ever read a book. He never did.

My father was so bad, you can't believe it. He was an embezzler against the family which gave him a job only because he married my mother. He was a teller in the bank. The reason he was a teller was because my mother got hot pants for him. This beautiful man who looks like Tyrone Power who comes from Kansas, Speed Welch. Bam! He comes in and she can't believe it. And when the dance is through they are married. My grandfather is already dead. My grandfather would have seen this. That this man was a phony. But the kid came up to her and he was very handsome and very sharp.

My mother had $100,000, American big ones, in 1922. She was rich. I mean super-rich. And her friends were all superrich. Well, Lew Welch, my father, was a poor man who was very clever. And he really loved my mother, there is no question about that. This is a very interesting part of it. My mother really loved that man and that man really loved my mother. And the stories that go to prove it are really intricate and probably not worth going into. Suffice it to say that I know I was not born into a wedlock of hate.

This should be put into this. It is very important. I went to the loony bin when I was fourteen months old.

DM: I don't understand.

LW: I know you don't. It is the world's record. Even among my beat generation friends. I have the world's record. I copped out, I went crazy, split, I said, "Forget it! No, I don't want it," when I was fourteen months old. I'll tell you why.

It's a very simple thing. I refused to eat. And I would have died unless I got really strict attention. My mother was a twenties flapper, pretty, and high-style, who had little breasts and probably taped *them* down. Anyway, there wasn't enough milk and to this day, when I go into rages like I do, she'll say, "You used to look like that when you were a little baby. You used to pound on my chest and turn red and scream." She made feeding so awful I cracked up.

When I was six, I remember her sticking enormous bowls of oatmeal in front of me. It was disgusting. She'd scream, "Eat! Eat!" I still have trouble eating. I'm a classic case of the alcoholic with an eating problem. To this day I suck on the tit of the bottle. I try to control it but the scars are very deep.

It's awful to be born to a rich, selfish shiksa. It wasn't her fault, but whose bad habits of mind are purely their own? It's still awful. Growing up was something I'd sure never want to do, that way, ever again.

Let's get out to the positive part of it. All I have done correctly in literature, if I have done anything correctly, was done because I resisted a terrible mother who was the absolute form of Kali, death. Even her pets die inside of a year or two. And then you can see why I praise the planet so highly. Why I take other goddesses.

The thing is that my need for the woman, my mother, was very deep and frustrated. So I hated my mother very strongly for not being able to give it to me. Though she tried. God, did she try! But maybe because of this I admire all of the great feminine traits in the world, such as the mountains, or my present wife, Magda. I am especially sensitive to how beautiful it is when it comes.

So this is why if I sound like I am exaggerating

about Mount Tamalpais, it is just that I have taken
Mount Tamalpais as my goddess in a very real way,
like a priest takes a vow. I mean it.

I ask her, Mount Tamalpais, about this, about that,
and I listen to what she tells me. A lot of people
think I am being goofy about it, you know, or being
poetic about it, but I mean it. I really mean it and
the only way to say it is in the poetry. The praises.
Prayers.

How did I get out of it? When I was eleven years
old I wanted a pair of tennis shoes very badly. And
this was a way out of it. My mother explained to me
that I had very bad feet, because when I was in
kindergarten, that was in Santa Monica, she got in
the grips of some idiot who made a steel-trap shoe
that ruined my feet so bad . . . you know, if you put
anything into a cast long enough it becomes atrophied. When I was in the seventh grade, my feet
were atrophied because I had to wear high shoes. I
insisted on tennis shoes and there was a big scene
and luckily we were in a school where we had a good
coach. I was very fast. And we would run bare-
footed. We didn't have any shoes and I won. I was
the county champion at fifty yards in the sixth grade,
and I was really a small tad then. I really ran faster
than anybody else in the whole county and broke
my arches doing it. Because my mother had put my
feet in those iron shoes. But I won it anyway. Because
I took them off and did it. And when it got to be that
way, when my feet were really broken and I couldn't
walk, I had a confrontation with her and I won it.
And the doctor did what was needed.

I had to walk backward for the entire time I was
in the ninth grade. Backward, because I could not
walk any other way and I would not let my mother
give me another crutch. And there were exercises to
do, which I did, and my feet got fairly normal.

In Chicago, about 1954, I got a poem out of a dream I had. I often dream poems, and if everything is just right I can go back in there and dig the poem out by re-dreaming it. It is a poetic skill I'm proud of and on which I work very hard. I hope to be able to have a mind, finally, which has the thinking of sleep (which we call dreaming) and the thinking of waking (which we call thinking) be the same available thing.

I was dreaming, in Chicago, on a hot summer afternoon nap, that I was reading a book called *Expediencyitis*. Isn't that a great word? And the book was written by a German whose name I can't remember. The book was written as Cocteau writes, and as Wittgenstein, the form I feel is the finest form for the true mind transmission: the form is little paragraphs separated by dots, and the paragraphs have no obvious connection with one another, but the whole form finally comes through. You can see it in Cocteau's *Opium* and in Wittgenstein's *Philosophical Investigations* (originally his *Brown and Blue Books*) and in that book about Huang-Po— *Mind Transmission*. It's also in Stein's lectures and I hope, somewhat there already, in this piece we're doing here.

Anyway, I am dreaming I'm reading this perfect book, *Expediencyitis*, which has this perfect form and is very wise, and I realize, while dreaming, that this is not written by any German but is being dreamed by me, therefore written by me. I'm dreaming this thought about the dream. So it is so fascinating that, when I awake, I say to myself: "Let's go back in there and get some of that." And I rolled over and forced myself back into sleep and that dream, and came up with this:

Through the years of her speech
a persistent gong

told us how grief had
cracked the bell of her soul.

It was months before I realized this poem exactly
said what I felt about my mother's agony and her
language. When I wrote it down upon recovering the
dream, I had no idea what it meant.

3

LW: When you come into a new school, the first guy
that comes up to talk to you is the guy that is sus-
picious. If he has to come up to you and you are the
only new kid, then he can't be any good, can he?
The second thing that happens is that there are
games in the yard. And it turns out that I was gifted
with very swift legs. I could always hang back, play
very quiet. I have already rejected the first kid that
came up to me because you know he was no good
because he had to come up to the new kid. He
doesn't have any friends, so who the hell wants to
know him, right? Then there gets to be this day and
I remember it with really great pleasure.
   They had a game called Pom Pom Pull-away. It
was very simple. One guy is "it" and he stands in the
middle of the football field and everybody runs by
him and everybody he tags is also "it." And finally
everybody is "it" and there are a few people who try
to work through.

OK, I am the new kid. Nobody knows who I am and we are playing Pom Pom Pull-away and we have only an hour to do this. So there is a guy named "it" and everybody runs across the football field a couple of times and then everybody is on the football field and there are about fifteen of us, and I was one of them. And they say: "Who are you?" and I say: "I am Lew Welch."

And we ran through the next time and nobody could catch me. And we went through the next time and still nobody could catch me. I will never forget this triumph. This was a real triumph. Finally the entire school was "it." And I was the only guy that wasn't and nobody knew who I was. I made it three times through all of them and the coach came up and said: "Do you want to come out for football?" And I said: "Yeah." That's a true story. And I did it, man.

There was a very beautiful man named Robert Rideout who was a teacher in the seventh grade and he had a very simple thing going. He said, "If you ever like a book, you will probably like another book by the man that wrote it." He would lay books on us.

I must say this in defense of my mother. One of the best things she said to me was: "You know, all the knowledge of the world is in the library and I will show you how to use it." And she did. She took me to the library and we walked in and she showed me how the card catalog worked and she introduced me to the lady who worked there and I spent a very beautiful summer there and was very proud of it. Like I could really go up to the card catalog, look up books, get authors, pull the books off the shelves, and so on. It was too much, man.

DM: Did you teach yourself to read, or were you taught to read?

LW: No, like most of us, the real readers, it all happened accidentally. My mother was a very good reader . . . this is in defense of my mother. She was very good about that. She would always read us stories when we were very young. I started reading when I was five or six, because she sat us on her lap as she read, *Dr. Dolittle,* or whatever it was, and she would move her finger over the words, and I learned accidentally how to read. No, it wasn't accidentally. Not really. It was because of her good grace. She really loved books. So all blessings to her.

I am going to mention right out in my author's preface to my new book, *Ring of Bone* (Grove Press, 1971), you know, where it says: Thank you. I don't even know where he is now, but Robert Rideout was a seventh-grade teacher in El Cajon, California, and he had this little thing about how books were to be used.

I am on a pirate kick, so he gets me *Falcon of France.* Nordhoff and Hall wrote *Mutiny on the Bounty.* Hall was really a World War I pilot. Rideout had the sense to see that if the kid liked pirates, he would certainly like this. So then, bang! I go into all the World War I airplane books.

Rideout said: "Every time you read a book, write it down. Write down the author and tell whether you liked it or not." He had a five-star system. One star for bad, two, etc. You know what I did? I read 160 books in one year under Rideout. Most of them were about pirates or airplanes. He was too much.

He got me into Ernest Thompson Seton. He got me into all the Lassie books, the dog and animal bit. But Ernest Thompson Seton was a really important writer and Nordhoff and Hall were great. And, most of all Will James.

DM: When did you start reading poetry?
LW: Ha! Right then! In the middle of all this reading, I read "Trees" by Joyce Kilmer. I ran into and out of the pirate thing. I ran into and out of the

Ernest Thompson Seton thing. And suddenly I got into poetry, and believe it or not, it was Joyce Kilmer's "Trees" first, and more importantly, Robert Service. No kidding. This is true, man. That son of a bitch is a terribly good poet.

I got *Rhymes of a Red Cross Man* when I was about eleven years old. And when he talks about the man on the wire—I said: *"There!"* That was the great thing that drove me to poetry. Service never cheats. And his *On the Wire,* that man is festering on the wire and people are shooting at him and it is getting hot . . . whew! I got it! I got truth! So Robert Service is a super-American poet.

DM: No doubt about it. He is incredible. He is tremendous to read aloud to people.

LW: Right! When I was on my hermitage, and it really was a hermitage, we would sit and weep with bad sherry wine. Me and a bunch of bad-ass drunk Indians. And we would read a poem about a dog by Service and we would break up. It was relevant. It was truly relevant. I would like to have poetry be the kind of thing that a man can say with good friends in a mountain cabin. And Robert Service can do it.

DM: How did you become interested in language? For instance, you talk about your speed, being able to move . . . when did you realize that language was a way of moving too?

LW: That's a well-put question.

When you say something right, "with your finger on the throttle and your foot upon the pedal of the clutch," you are doing something in language that becomes almost abstract to most minds, but to my mind this is the supreme act.

The difference between the ordinary kind of language that we use every day and the language that we call poetry is very slim when we have great poets working. Example. Take Burns' "Loch Lomond." You think that's language and you can actually sing it.

But you don't realize how complicatedly the man has bent language in order for it to be said that way.

I would like to be the kind of singer that is respected by his tribe in the way Bobby Burns is respected. I would much rather have that kind of a feeling from my people than anything else I can think of.

What I would really like to do . . . say, wouldn't it be wonderful to write a song or a story that anybody would say, *"That* is art," on any given evening just because he loved the way it went? And that is what I want to do. And that is what I think poetry is about. And I think at times that some of my poetry has done that.

DM: Do you remember when you wrote your first poem. Can you remember what it was about?

LW: "Skunk Cabbage" was my first poem.

I began to be a poet at Reed College and one day I was walking around the pond they had there . . . a very lovely lake . . . and there is also a swamp behind it where you could get laid by your girl. I saw this thing and it was really weird. It was a skunk cabbage. I believe this was my first poem.

Slowly in the swamps unfold
great yellow petals of a
savage thing, a
tropic thing

While no stilt-legged birds watch,
no monkeys scream,
those great yellow petals
unfold.

Rank plant!

I really thought that then. I saw that then. That is when I started to be a poet.

The way I went to Reed College is a long story. I went to the war and got through it and that's not interesting. World War II. No, I didn't fight. It was just a big bummer. I tried very hard to fight. I wanted to be Errol Flynn. Let's get back to that later. I want to tell you how I got to Reed College and it takes about eight hours from one point to the other. I mean, like World War II was not interesting at all. A bummer.

I want to tell you what I feel about poetry. I can do it easily with a poem of mine.

I WANT THE WHOLE THING, THE MOMENT
    when what we thought was rock, or
        sea
    became clear Mind, and

  what we thought was clearest Mind really
    was that glancing girls, that
      swirl of birds . . .

    (all of that)

AND AT THE SAME TIME that very poem
    pasted in the florist window

(as Whalen's *I Wanted To Bring You This Jap Iris* was)
    carefully re-typed and
put right out there on Divisadero Street.

      just because the florist thought it
        pretty,

        that it might remind of love,
        that it might sell flowers . . .

The line

Tangled in Samsara!

4

LW: I want to get into that now. The thing about poetry that is usually wrong is that the people who tend to be writing it are not poets. They don't know what their tribe is speaking and they don't have anything to talk about themselves.

I met William Carlos Williams in 1950. I had graduated in June and waited all summer, with a fine redheaded girl, to meet him in September. I remember I put all my poems together, I was only about twenty-four, and added great long explanations, so I'd be ready for him.

Whalen, Snyder, and I were asked by the school, Reed was really a groovy place then, to go meet him at the airport. After all, we were the poets of Reed, and the faculty was sort of embarrassed about it all. So we got him into his hotel and rapped with him, it was like meeting a saint, a really important man, and he came on like a Middle Western hick, really, shy and everything. I always think of him as looking like President Truman.

He was so sweet and humble and we loved him so much. He had saved our lives. And when we told him how he had, truly, defeated T. S. Eliot, he was really touched. That young men, poets, would come to him and say he had won the battle of his life.

We took him to our pad, where Whalen and Snyder

and I lived, and we played poetry games and talked and we gave him our stuff. And when he gave his reading at Reed, he began by saying, "It's good to be in a place where they will give a degree for a thesis on Gertrude Stein." I was so overwhelmed, after nobody wanted me to do the Stein thesis, and then my hero said that! He was the first poet I had met. He asked me to visit him in Rutherford. Again, I was overwhelmed. But I did it. I went to see him at his home maybe three or four times. I was pure mind transmission. I really became a poet only because of Williams. Williams and Gertrude Stein.

One day we were waiting for the dinner, served as "supper" in New Jersey at two in the afternoon, and Williams invited me upstairs to wash up. On the way we stopped at a three-drawer file cabinet and he said, "That's my autobiography in there." And then he took me into a large room with a big oak table in the middle of it, and on the table was a funky old typewriter. Very neat. No clutter at all. And he said, to *me*, the punk, "This is where I work."

I felt like I was somebody in the baby trade, that I had come to investigate a foster father, and that he was saying: "See, I am raising it with love." I could hardly eat.

Years later he wrote to me: "I knew you were cracking up in New York, but it's like a concentration camp, one look of recognition and you too are done in. Thanks for the book. Sometimes it's a long time coming."

I had sent him *Wobbly Rock,* and he was into his fourth or fifth stroke, dying, and I wanted to thank him for what he had done for me.

Maybe five meetings altogether, but the result is total mind transmission, when the man is that great, and I hope I carry it well.

You have to know what the tribe is speaking and you have to have something to talk about yourself. This is a two-part argument. Let's take the first part.

You have to have a sense of what the tribe is speaking. This takes ear training. You have to go out into the street and listen to the way people talk. You have to really listen to the kind of things that people say. You have to listen to the birds that are in the air, the helicopters, the big rush of jets. . . . Listen to this, you can't even talk in my living room without the din of it. You have to have your ears open. You have to have your goddamn ears open or you are not going to be a poet. Or you are not going to be a writer of any importance whatsoever.

I am sick and tired of all these punk kids trying to tell me how sad they are every time they walk through a park. Come on. Step one.

We have two things . . . you have to hear what is. You have to hear how your mother talked. You have to hear how your mother talked in a way that is so straight that it will almost kill you. Not only what she said, but how the language moved in what she said. And how the language affected the people around her. Because that is what is going to affect you. And you have to know what the people in the town talk like. How it is said. You have to know it so perfectly that you can never ever make an error. Even Hemingway made errors, and we must not, if we are poets, ever make an error. It is a very precise art and a strong and a good one. I die behind it . . . its strength and its purpose.

I had the privilege of seeing a poem of mine pasted in the No Name Bar window. I was asked by the owner of that bar to partake in a small demonstration to protest against the misuse of the beautiful area that the city of Sausalito is. It's being badly misused.

You have this gorgeous beach that is nothing but asphalt and parking meters. So we had this demonstration and it was really touching to me, and a source of great gratification, to be asked by an innkeeper in one's own village to partake in such a thing because of the fact that I am a poet. He wanted me to write a prayer and speak it. And I did. And then he published it . . . it's just a little short poem. We published it by going to the public library and for a dime apiece Xeroxed it until we got forty copies and we gave them to the press, and gave them to the people in the crowd, and they could read behind me. And then it was pasted in the window of the bar for the people on the street to see.

SAUSALITO TRASH PRAYER

Sausalito,
Little Willow,
Perfect Beach by the last Bay
        in the world,
None more beautiful,
Today we kneel at thy feet
And curse the men who have misused you.

I think that poetry should be at least as lively as Robert Burns is. Where it can be used by the tribe in moments of need. When the chips are down, it's the turn of the new year, and you are drunk and you can't even move, but you still sing *Auld Lang Syne*.

DM: I remember, back a few years ago, you were involved with trying to organize a fund to feed the poets of America. . . . You were planning to put out a magazine called *Bread* that would contain material showing how hard it is to survive economically as a poet in America . . .

LW: A big organization called Bread, Inc. All I would have needed was ten million dollars and then we would be able to support all the poets that would be in America, ever. I figured ten million dollars would be the capital. You would have a half-million a year, five hundred thousand bucks and also a hospital fund so poets could have babies and fix their wives' teeth and the other things that we need. The rest would be doled out . . .

See, the trouble with most grants is that the grants are either for a book that is going to be written, or not written, or it's for going to Italy and doing something. Nobody just gives you bread. I don't need any grants. I know what I am going to do next year. What I need is four thousand dollars! Like maybe I'll just sit here and spend it all on bourbon, but that's my goddamn right. If I am a poet I need bread to go, just like a car. You have to put gas in it. So that was the idea behind Bread, Inc.

The fortunes of life have gone in such a way that I now have a way to get bread by myself, but it's very time-consuming and it's a big drag. But at least I have it.

DM: What work do you do now to earn a living?

LW: I work on the docks as a longshoreman's clerk. And I also get fees for going around and reading poetry. I ask for $500 and I get about $350. I work for as cheap as $100 if it is close, like Davis. At American River I went for $100 because it is in Sacramento. In fact, in the last two years, I have covered every part of the U. of California except UCLA.

I want poetry to be as useful as singing The *Star Spangled Banner* at a baseball game. I want it to be right in there. It is really strange to see that's possible, even in a culture as vulgar as America. It has happened. Like Phil Whalen's poem was really pasted in that florist's window. I didn't make that up. And my poem was really stuck up in a bar window.

I got two free drinks from a guy in Riverside just a few weeks ago. Before the poetry reading there, I asked the guys that were driving me from the airport to the reading to stop at a bar and we would all have a drink together. And as we had a drink, I got all excited . . . I am getting ready for the reading and I happen to mention this to a very groovy bartender why I was in town, and would he like to have a book of mine. He said: "Why sure." And I said, "You can't have it unless I can read it out loud, right here." And he got very nervous because he expected some gloomy poem . . . "I-love-the-night" bunch of bullshit to come out of me. Here it was, eleven in the morning and who was ready for poetry? Who was ready for poetry in a bar in Riverside at eleven A.M. in the morning?

And I read *Courses* to him from start to finish, and he broke up. He thought it was the funniest thing he had ever heard. So I laid the book on him and said, "See, I work. Like Bobby Burns worked. I am trying to get the poem back into the bar." And he said, "That's a good idea. You should hear most of the shit these people talk around here!"

It could easily follow from such a position that, therefore, poetry would be quite mundane, watered down, made popular. Pop art instead of great art. Now I think that Bobby Burns wrote as fine a set of lyrics as any poet ever wrote. Or even more heavily, probably the greatest poet that ever lived was Milarepa, the great Tibetan Buddhist. All of his teachings are in the form of songs. They are poems that he sang out loud to his students, his disciples, the people in the town.

The poetry of Homer, after all, are simply the songs of a blind old man in a time when there weren't printed books. Men would go around and tell the kings what their history was. Chaucer is the same thing. Chaucer is the man who made poetry of the streets, just as Han-Shan's poetry would be scribbled on shithouse walls. . . . People found them on the rocks. Han-Shan wrote them on the rocks on the mountains. People would run down to town and say: "Han-Shan's written a new poem!" They would write it on the walls.

Po-Chui, the great Chinese bard . . . his poetry was memorized by all the harlots in China, and was sung by all the whores and pimps. I am not talking about writing down something. I believe if a poem is really well made, it can be strong enough to stand inside the general din of the speaking world.

We do a lot of talking, don't we? And the best talking we call poetry.

If the poem is made right it will sit well in any room. Now I believe this is the starkest, most unmundane standard for a poet to set for himself and his work. The opposite is . . . you take a guy like Rod McKuen, he is not a poet at all. He is not doing anything that is even interesting. Contrast him to a real poet like Bob Dylan whose poems are in every living room.

I remember when I read my taxicab poem in a pool hall I used to play in when I was a cabdriver. I got to know these guys very well. This is a problem in America because America is such a vulgar place. I mean vulgar in the real sense, like coarse. If you are a cabdriver and you have cabdriver friends and they finally get to know and like you and then you say: "I am a poet" . . . they instantly think you are a goddamn queer. It is very hard to be a virile man going about his life when the main part of your life is being a poet. The main part of my life, the part I hold closest to my sense of self, is Lew Welch, the poet. I am also a father and a lover and a husband and a worker and a good shot or whatever it is that I think about myself, but always riding over it is: I am really Lew Welch, poet. Now you find you have to say to your cabdriving, pool-playing buddies that you are a poet sooner or later. You have to tell them, you have to let them in on it, you have to. Otherwise you are cheating them of your friendship. And when you do, you get this: "Mm-mm, uh-uh, oh, yeah . . ."

Anyway, I told them at this pool game. I said, "By the way, do you know that I am a poet? If you don't mind, I would like to read you one." And I read them *After Anacreon.* And they stopped chalking their cues, and they stopped playing and they really started listening. And when I finished, they said: "Goddamn, Lewie, I don't know whether or not that is a poem, but that is the way it *is* to drive a cab."

I said, "Thanks, I am just testing it."

Now, Po-Chui used to do that too. He was a very great poet that used to have a peasant lady who was illiterate yet very very smart. She was a peasant lady who ran a good garden down the road and he would go and engage her in conversation. And then he would dump the poem on her and if she didn't recognize that he had just said a poem, he figured that he had written it right. If she had a little "huh?" about it or something; if it seemed awkward to her or wrong, somehow ungraceful, then Po-Chui would go back and fix it. At the same time, that very poem would have more literary references in it for the literate reader than we can imagine today. Po-Chui is a real master at this, a super T. S. Eliot. He can put more echoes of old poems into four or five lines than any Chinese ever did before or after, and that is really something. He tested it against this lady who never read a poem in her life or wanted to. That's a standard, and that's the way I feel about that standard.

Let's get a little more technical about it. Talking about it like a poet talks to another poet.

You have a sense of language where language is

held as a music, where that music is the sound of a taut soul singing. You have this kind of sense of language for some mysterious reason. It is a mystery. I don't understand it. There are people who write and sometimes make a poem. But then a weird thing happens to those of us who have this sense of language with this kind of intensity. It causes us to train ourselves as carefully as a flutist will. It is very very close to music where you have to learn how to practice and practice. You have to learn how to shave the reed just right—you have to learn how to breathe just right . . .

The poem should be able to be spoken so that the performance is just as much a part of it. . . . In other words, what you do when you write down a poem is that you are transcribing a voice. You are not learning how to read the poem, you are learning how to write the song. For me, poetry is the sound of a man in words. And it partakes of song, of chanting, of prayer, of all the things we do when we really intensify language.

Learning the art of poetry also becomes learning the art of hearing. Ear training and voice training, just as surely as a musician does it.

I have always respected Rexroth's opinions on these matters. I have never found him to be incorrect. He put it this way once. He said he likes translating poetry when the muse isn't with him. He was going back to the old thing . . . that the muse wasn't there. You haven't got a poem of your own and you are getting restless. You are saying, "My God, I am a poet and I have no poem. What will I do today?" You know how awful it is? Rexroth says, "Keep your hand in by making translations." He says, "More often than not, halfway through the translating, a poem comes out." The muse . . . that crazy little chick running around and rapping at a bunch of idiots who don't understand what she is saying . . .

and she goes over and sees you are working very hard and she says, "Sweet old Lewie," and goes over and says, "Bark," in your ear, and pretty soon, bang! you have a poem. And the translation falls by, or it comes out close enough to the guy so that you say *After Anacreon* or *After William Blake*.

It's fun to translate English poets. For example, like Yeats has a poem that could be a very great poem, but he wrote it badly because he took the wrong meter. Yeats was really kind of meter-dumb. He is, I think, the greatest English-writing poet of the century, but he had a funny trick ear.

5

LW: The art of poetry, in my mind, is connected with the art of music, because in my life it was. I some-times ask myself: When did you start being a poet? I remember when I was four years old running in to my mother: "You should have heard what Milton the gardener said," I said, " 'I ain't got nothing.' " And I laughed because I thought that was the funniest thing I had ever heard. My mother had a very quick ear for language up to a point and she could see that that was a very unusual thing for a four-year-old boy to hear. To hear a funny word structure and to laugh at it. But my mother took it to mean that I was a natural scholar, or that I knew right from wrong. I wasn't hearing "wrong," I was hearing what he said.

Like, "can't hardly" always hits my ear with a very funny ring.

You see, the stuff of poetry insists that you have this kind of sense, somehow or other, and it is quite a mystery. It's just there or it isn't there. There is no way of teaching it. There *is* a way of honing it down, refining it, sharpening it up.

John Handy told me that after a few weeks he could play horn, alto sax, he already knew the clarinet, almost perfectly, not to his ear, but to everybody else's ear. He had to go into the hard work of it. Practicing scales over and over again. Long slow tones.

The second thing was that we had a jug, which I still have on my desk, to remind me of my sources. And on this jug is a little poem that I think was the start of it. It goes:

Do the work that's nearest
though it is dull at whiles,
helping when you meet them
lame dogs over stiles.

I found myself at twelve or thirteen reading that poem on the jug and thinking that those people needed some help. It's almost like a parody of Thelonious Monk. "Helping when you meet them" . . . what a funny meter! I'd see it every morning. The jug was on what my mother called a Welsh dresser, which is a piece of furniture that you put in the dining room and display all your pretty plates on.

DM: Can you remember your first interest in music, specifically in jazz?
LW: It was so early that I can't even figure it out. My mother reports once that I was about three or four and I was walking through a store in San Diego and I was singing something I had just heard on the

phonograph or the radio. I had remarkable retention. And I could sing right in tune and with great pleasure.

I did play clarinet, but never had the patience to learn an instrument. I've always been a very impatient person, and this business of embouchure, fingering, the little black notes, always stopped me. I started on clarinet, accordion, piano, bass, and now my music is entirely singing.

I used to call myself the best jug player in America but I realized just yesterday that I wasn't. I was playing with an Okie chick that really knows that kind of music. Do you know Peter Coyote's old lady with a tattoo on her tit? She's the best Jew's-harp player in the whole world! God, she's good! I was playing with her and she said, "You don't play jug, you play bottle." And it's true. Jug players play big three-quart ceramic instruments that have a tuba sound to them. But I play a glass bottle which has a high frequency and a high resonance. The best general jug, believe it or not, is a quart Coca-Cola bottle. Something about the curves in it, I guess.

I remember that the only way my mother could make me wake up happy was to put on Cootie Williams. I just loved Cootie Williams! Do you know, he played a trumpet in such a way that you could *taste* the notes. Really chewy. Chu Berry I dug. He had that bite, that mouth thing going, like Hawkins did. So it was people like Cootie Williams, Hawkins, Prez, and of course, the real capper was Charlie Parker. Goddamn! That man astounds me to this day! When I listen to his records, I still can't believe it.

DM: It's sad to note that only a small percentage of Parker's total record output is available in his country.

LW: Is that so? I wouldn't doubt it. America is so vulgar! Americans just can't see heroes!

I had the great privilege of hearing that man "live"

every single night for nearly two years. Because I went to the trouble to go hear him. The blessing was that he was there. I was also very grateful that somehow or other my hearing and my sense of the importance of this man was such that I availed myself of the opportunity.

I was at the U. of Chicago in '51, '52, '53, and '54 and at that time Charles was damn near dead. I really enjoy calling him *Charles* Parker. There is something about "Charlie" that doesn't fit the man. He was Charles. He was dying and none of us realized it.

He was working in a little joint on 63d Street in Chicago and all of his side musicians were high-school kids. Just a thrown-together band: a piano, bass, drum, and Parker. That's all. The kids would be eighteen, nineteen, twenty, maybe twenty-one . . . if they weren't old enough they would fake their age or something. But really nowhere. I mean the kind of group you would expect to find in an after-hours joint in San Francisco. Really dedicated, really young musicians who knew who the hell Parker was. Boy did they know! They just played their asses off.

And he would come up after a set . . . oh, I remember him so well! He always wore double-breasted brown suits—God, or a brown double-breasted gabardine coat with blue pinstripe pants and bad shoes, just terrible. The cat just didn't give a fuck how he looked, he just didn't care at all. And his horn always hanging from his neck, and he had these funny walleyes . . . the one eye was high and to the outside . . .

He would come after a set, you know, one of those fantastic tunes [*Lew scats "Scrapple from the Apple."*] and the kids are trying to stay in there with him, and they are staying as best they can because they know who they are playing with. They know it. (I'd like to run into a couple of those kids now. I bet they are big guys now. Real heavy.) After the set was over—and here was everyone, a bunch of Okies in a Chicago bar giving you so much *crap*. No one was even listening, man . . . just nothing going on . . . there would be maybe eight people there: me and seven pimps and whores. Weird, man, because it was really a down Chicago bar scene. One of the places was called The Beehive. Charles Parker revolved around four joints within six blocks on 63d Street, which is a famous old jazz street. Apparently he had a good contact for his heroin. That is the reason why he stayed there. Because he had a big name, Jesus, he could have made three or four thousand a week!

You know who he reminded me of? The only person I have ever met that reminded me of Charles Parker was Jack Spicer. They were the same man. They were just hell-bent on self-destruction. They were both six feet plus and heavy. They were big and strong. Jesus, Charles Parker had hands like a fucking farmer! Big hands. He had a working body and it turned all into mind at a terrible price. They were very similar men and they both had the same approach to their art.

Parker used to get up after a set and walk over to the piano player and he would be so sweet . . . his horn hanging from his neck like a big necklace. He was big enough, he was really a strong man, his horn just hung and swung around. He didn't hold it like other guys do. And he leaned over and showed the kid how the chords should have gone. And the kid would sit there like: "Oh, yeah, oh yeah . . . of course . . . B flat 7th . . . oh, B 9th minor . . . wow! . . ." And the next time Charles would say: "Let's do *Salt Peanuts*." And these tremendous tempos he would lay on these poor kids. Tremendous tempos that he would take with great ease and brilliance . . .

The great breakthrough for me was of a structural nature. My ear began to hear things in terms of structure, not in terms of meaning. Almost as far back as I can remember, I was hearing structures. The big breakthrough came when I was freaking out as a twenty-year-old college student will freak out. I had this dear teacher who understood everything, I thought, and I had to see him.

I was really freaking out . . . I was on a $600-a-year track scholarship, wearing the saddle shoes, a fraternity boy at Stockton Junior College. And I have all that going for me . . . fraternity houses where I can't get laid . . . my head's breaking . . . and I had to talk to this man who is named James Wilson and is now a teacher at San Francisco State . . . a very dedicated teacher, one of those rare men who regards teaching as an art. He really got through to me and I had to talk to him. I don't know what I wanted to say to him . . . you know how it is when you are that young. I go into his office and he is not there. His desk is very littered and there are lots of books and most of them are open and I decide I am going to sit there and wait until he comes back, no matter how long it takes.

I picked up a book called *Three Lives* by Gertrude Stein and I read *Melanctha*. And I became a writer. It's the damnedest thing. It's like Malraux reports in *The Voices of Silence:* "We are brought to art by an artist. We are not brought to art by a natural wonder." I read *Melanctha* and the impression was really wonderful. She is not so hard to understand. Everyone has been telling me that Gertrude Stein was "A rose is a rose is a rose . . ."

DM: You had been writing, hadn't you?

LW: No, I was only twenty then. Oh, yes, I was sports editor for the paper. I did all the writing for the tribe. When they needed somebody, it was: "Lew,

will you do this, Lew would you make a speech?" I
always did it, but I thought of myself as a painter, a
singer, and a track star. I was a voracious reader. I
never read less than four books a week since I was
about nine. And then in college I ran the 440 in 49.7
seconds.

Suddenly, reading *Melanctha* I felt as though I
had been invited to a very distinguished party, a
weekend party in the country, and at this party there
was Shakespeare, Poe, Stein, Joyce, Dickens, Chaucer,
all of the people that I had admired. And because of
Stein's story *Melanctha*, it was like an invitation.
"Why don't you come out to the country and spend a
weekend with us?"

I came to that house and I came with great
humbleness. And I didn't say a word. I just listened.
I listened for a long time, and it was a good long
party. Now I am forty-three and I do most of the
talking. After all, they are tired, but the same people
are there. And that is who I am talking to and it is
wonderful to want to listen once in a while. I don't
know how I see them. Do I see them as a monkey in
a zoo with the visitors, or what? But I must do my
talking, my poetry, to them, the hosts of the party.
That is my real audience.

Anyway, there was this moment in my life reading
this one story and I suddenly said: "Goddamn, writing is not only a good thing to do, it is very easy. The
thing you have to do is to put your words down
absolutely true like Gertrude Stein is doing here." It
wasn't so much that I loved the story better than other
stories, or that I liked the writing more, it was a
moment of revelation. A vision. The mystical part,
the mystery of it, is contained in an experience like
that.

That was my presence at the great garden party.
I worked for them for nearly ten years to learn ex-

actly what Gertrude Stein had going for her and why. And I still believe that Gertrude Stein is probably the best writer if you just want to take writing as a supreme exquisite art. Nobody ever did it as purely as Gertrude Stein, because everybody gets the story in the way somehow or other, or gets themselves in the way. She really went word, word, word, word, word. You know how musicians talk about Mozart? Well, that is the way Stein is as a writer in my mind.

I know writers I prefer to read now, but I don't know of anybody who can write better than Gertrude Stein, ever. She is just a supreme master of this business of getting what is in your head out of your head and into words. Writing as opposed to storytelling. Making a *poem* instead of "making it up." Anderson I respect at the same level and Hemingway too, but I really think that Gertrude was right, that Hemingway learned from Stein, not vice versa. She also said: "But I have a weakness for Hemingway." She saw that. She also said that, and she's right: "The first person that ever wrote an American sentence was Sherwood Anderson."

Sherwood Anderson is another very wrongly placed person in the literary fable. This man was a real giant and you never hear anybody talking about him anymore. I think Gertrude was a little wrong about him being first, because the opening of Mark Twain's *Life on the Mississippi* has, for me, the first American sentences. One after the other. Hundreds of them and they are all perfect and big.

DM: What about Thoreau?

LW: Thoreau, Melville, Hawthorne, Emerson, and Whitman . . . they are very great Americans and great writers but they didn't write in this funny diction that has now become the major language of the earth. But Twain did, and Stein did, and Sherwood Anderson did, and Hemingway did.

But Hemingway did it as if he had heard Sherwood Anderson and Stein do it so perfectly that he could not miss. No, he wasn't cheating any more than Shakespeare was cheating when he came onto his Elizabethan English because Marlowe and Sidney had done so much hard work that he could do it easily without thinking about it. He didn't cheat. In other words, it gave him the strength of confidence he needed in order to write it truly in the way that he spoke. I don't think Hemingway could have done it by himself. It was Stein, Twain, and Sherwood Anderson that rapped it in his ear and gave him the freedom to work with it.

You see, Marlowe made up the line that Shakespeare was free to use. This doesn't put Hemingway down to say it at all. It just places him in another order of creativity.

I find myself in this role. There is a lot of hard work that I don't have to do because men like William Carlos Williams did it for me. Stein did it for me. Also Hemingway did it for me and Sherwood Anderson did it for me. I find that when I read Whitman I feel I am reading a translation . . .

You see, you have a tree and you have the real limbs and leaves and always you have the sports. Now at times these sports are the most prized. They are really beautiful. I think Robert Duncan's work is very beautiful. But it is utterly useless and will not have any heirs. And it will not go anywhere and it came from part of the trunk that I don't understand —but I respect it. It's really a strong piece of the tree. But it is a sport. It is a sucker that comes off the side. I don't know or care where it comes from.

T. S. Eliot would be in the same class. He had nothing to do with English literature at all. He is a sport off the side of it. While T. S. Eliot is fumbling around with his imitations of seventeenth-century sermons, the real work is being done by Hart Crane, William Carlos Williams, Fitzgerald, E. E. Cummings,

Gertrude Stein, Hemingway. Emily Dickinson is right there in the heartwood of the tree, so is Rexroth and Patchen and Miller. But not Pound, and certainly not Eliot.

The thing about the sucker, the sport, was that Eliot captured the imagination of so many people and made so many people look away from the real tree for so long. Eliot didn't say one thing pertinent to the twentieth-century. He simply is a recording of the best of the seventeenth-century sermon writers. Where the hell is the twentieth-century? His language is an absolute failure. Pound's language is even worse. I love Pound, but . . .

Those who seek to find poetry in the library, as Duncan and Eliot do, are ultimately doomed to failure. Duncan's language at a cocktail party is very lively. He is wonderful, but why the hell can't he get it into his poetry? He doesn't get it in there and therefore his poetry is dead.

Robin Blaser suffers from the same thing. Robin Blaser is one of the most erudite, witty, charming, good men that I have ever known and I can't understand why he uses poetry like some kind of shield between himself and reality. He uses it like I use chess in my life. I play chess as well as Robin writes poetry. He writes exquisite things that don't matter at all. There is no matter in them.

I find myself very uncomfortable talking against Duncan because I don't want to talk against Duncan, you know what I mean? But it evolves into an example, because he is so strong. He is so strong in doing whatever he is doing. But whatever he is doing does not, finally, matter.

6

LW: Let's get to the mystery. As I see it, it is like this. A vision is what you see with the mind's eye; which is to say, a vision is what you see. Of course, we see everything with the mind's eye, don't we? And the word "seer" is simply see-er. A person who sees.

We talked about how there are people who have an absurdly tense understanding of the way that language moves, and we call them poets. But then there are some people who have that gift and don't have anything to say. Like W. H. Auden would be one. He is just impeccable in his ability to handle word problems, yet he hasn't ever said one interesting thing to us, nor has Eliot, where William Blake really did.

Now a vision is what you see with the mind's eye; which is to say, a vision is what you see. A seer is a man who can see things that others cannot see. He is Prometheus, a man who goes into the void and brings back something and shows it to you, so that that kind of void is forever illuminated. After he has done that, anybody can look into that void and they can see it because the man brought it back. He illuminates something that anyone *could* see, but they don't see it. He does it some way. He paints it, he dances it, he writes it down.

Blake put it his way: "I do not distrust my corporal or vegetative eye any more than I would distrust a window for its sight. I look through it, not with it." That is the source of vision. That is a man who *sees*. A vision is what you see with the mind's eye, which is to say, a vision is what you see.

In my life I have never found a need to wonder about whether or not there is a god, let alone believe in it. The whole idea of another power has always seemed to me the most outrageously unnecessary and dangerous human idea that ever was. Yet, I have always worshiped this planet, which is, of course, another power.

There is something that is not us, right? Now for me, it is this earth that I stand on, these trees, this sweet air, the lovely water I drink, the fish that swim in it . . . all of this is a source of endless wonder. But it is the see-er in us who, as Stein put it, can "know themselves knowing it." We are the poets. When I was six years old, I used to take my bicycle to the ocean because my household was filled with very nervous women and I had to get out of there and my friends were nowhere, just kick-the-can bullshit friends . . . so I would go to the ocean and sit on an ocean rock and sit for hours and get all the sound of that ocean and pick those mussels and eat them raw —knowing that they are going to "poison you . . . impossible to eat them, you better not eat them . . ." fuck it! And I taught myself how to swim in it, and rub sand on my arms, and I figured out how to catch minnows with a little orange juice strainer, which I did because I was that patient. I didn't get very many, but I got them. And I saw an octopus as big as a coffee cup, a real octopus, and I got him and I put him in the tub and I looked at him and I said: "Shit, I am not going to take you home, baby." And I put him back, but I got him. That was my god, and still is my god, and I really deeply believe that if it can be that simple a god for everybody, than all the troubles we have would go away.

When you start talking to me about trinities and Christs, and virgin births, and saints, and Buddhas, like, forget it, man. That's all words. That's all shit, shit. That's trash. That's mind trash. Because it is right there under your feet, see? And it is not only your feet and your eyes that let you "know yourself knowing it." It's God.

Those are visions. They are things that you can see. You can see them. They are not special states of mind, although when I see them at times, the ecstasies get to the point that it is physically painful. I actually writhe like I am in a fit and I weep and I bellow. And that is the source of my poems. And I don't write from any other source, because the rest of it is just shit, trash. Mind trash.

You read poems by people who are always crying about how their girl left them or some kind of crap. I got a poem the other day from a student. A very nice poem about the moon. He had some good things in it.

It looked like he really looked at it a little. A little bit. Then he looked inside his own squirmy gut and he said: "Oh, it is sad!" He puts it in Spanish that the moon is sad. What a goddamn cop-out lie! The moon is not sad! When I look at that moon, I get so high, I blow my mind. Now don't tell me the moon is sad, because it isn't sad. Even Shelley wasn't that bad!

These ecstasies that I suffer have been suffered by every real poet that ever lived. And if you can't know them, you probably don't have a source strong enough to write a poem from.

You know my poem called *Ring of Bone?* I will let you in on a little secret. Here's what really happened.

I had to leave Lenore Kandel because she was corny and our life was not getting on together because of that. I have an exquisite kind of fineness to my life that she could not meet. She could not meet the other stuff that I needed desperately with perfection. She was a perfect helpmate. A goddamn good wife. But I didn't need it. I needed some other goddamn thing.

By this time I am thirty-eight, I am no punk anymore. It is really hurting. And how can you give up the most beautiful girl in San Francisco, who you need? But I had to go. I had to split and I remember the split. It was really wild. She is weeping at the top of the stairs and I am weeping at the bottom of the stairs and like there are no words left. And we are both poets. And she knows I've got to leave, yet she really doesn't know why.

Ferlinghetti loaned me his cabin in Big Sur. I went to him and said: "Look, man, it's really freak-city time. Can I borrow your cabin?"

He's beautiful that way. Sure. And bang, here's the key. OK, so down I go. I take enough groceries to last about two weeks, and a typewriter, and a lot of paper, and I just thrashed around in it. And one day, I got it.

I woke up after a wine drunk—I had brought a lot of red wine with me—I woke up about three in the afternoon and I saw it.

I saw myself
a ring of bone
in the clear stream
of all of it

and vowed
always to be open to it
that all of it
might flow through

and then heard
"Ring of bone" where
ring is what a
bell does.

And in the middle of it I got an erection, and put
my dick out the open window and I came without
even touching it. And that's the kind of ecstasies I
am talking about. It's like that old joke, you know,
a girl has a cunt that is too big and you say it is like
sticking your prick out the window and fucking the
world. That was it. I stuck my prick out and I fucked
the world.

And I freaked out. And I knew I am not kidding
now. I didn't make this up. I had to recover that
experience and I made this neat tight little poem out
of it. If I didn't have the chops now after twenty
years of hard work getting the chops down, I couldn't
capture it. People read that poem and they see and
sense a strange power. And they can't figure out why.

Now you heard the vision and now you have heard
the poem. Now these two things are terribly important. Without the practice I could not have captured it. I would have said: "I sure had a bad freak-
out in Big Sur, David. I think I had better go to
Langley Porter."

But if you are a poet, you can snag it, put it down
and then you look at the poem, and then you look at
your wet dick, and you look at the earth you just
came on, and you say, "Goddamn, it is all right, isn't
it?" You get a big up out of it. And I am *that* crazy.

It's the vision brought back. And it is not the

vision either. The poem is not the vision. The vision is the source of the poem. The poem is the chops, but the real chops are being able to go across that river and come back with something that is readable.

The ecstasies get to a point where they are usually unbearable. That one was on wine and despair. *Wobbly Rock* was done on despair. Period. And rain. We are in a drug era now. Everybody asks you, "Like what did you do it on?" Well, you do it cold sometimes. When ecstasies hit me, they hit me so hard sometimes that I wouldn't even entertain the idea of taking so much as a drink of wine, if it would mess with it.

The danger is that you begin to like them very much. The ecstasies. You require that every day you have one. This is, of course, a drag. No one could survive it. It is really debilitating. As Saints Teresa and John pointed out, as Huang-Po does. All the big mystics have pointed out that ecstasies are dangerous. They really are. I mean they are all right, and it is certainly wrong to deny yourself ecstasies if you happen to be available to them. Apparently, some people are not available to ecstasies. . . .

Summer, 1969

Michael McClure

1

MM: I came to San Francisco for two reasons. One: I was pursuing Joanna and two: I came here to take classes from Mark Rothko and Clifford Styll. When I arrived I found out that they had left the year before.

The mystique of abstract expressionism fascinated me. I would have painted had I taken classes from them, but I never really thought of myself as a painter. It was that I was experiencing what the painters were experiencing at that time.

DM: This was your fourth year of college?

MM: Yes. I graduated from San Francisco State. The year before I spent at the University of Arizona. All that I took there that I can remember was German and the Short Story. Oh, I also took an advanced Painting class and some Advanced Anthropology. Both classes were very interesting to me.

DM: When did you discover the work of William Blake?

MM: Very early. I was writing poems in the style of

Blake when I was seventeen. After high school I finished writing the pictographic poems I told you about—although they became less and less pictographic and more and more formal vers libre. Then I discovered Blake.

I bought the collected poems of Blake and Donne because somebody had recommended Donne to me. I couldn't read Donne, but I discovered those unbelievable poems of Blake. In the process of that I also discovered Milton. And between Blake, Yeats, and Milton I felt challenged to teach myself metric; to teach myself stanzaic patterns and shapes of poetry, like the sonnet and the villanelle.

I wrote very little in college and not much of it did I care for. I suppose it was a hermetic period. It was like a very long silent meditation on forms.

I also idealized what Dylan Thomas was doing. And I was terrifically impressed with Roethke.

I was writing poems in the manner of Blake. A cross between Blake and Baudelaire and at the same time learning forms like the Petrarchan sonnet, the ballad, the villanelle, the sestina.

It was very hard for me to write a sonnet. I might spend several weeks on a sonnet and then wait several weeks before I wrote another poem. I was very intent on having the meter correct, following the voice.

As for Blake, I used to dream I was Blake!

DM: So there was Blake, Yeats, and Milton?

MM: Yes, all about the same time.

DM: What a rich panoply of teachers!

MM: Yes. And I wasn't alone in this. There were five or six of us waiting and we fed each other intellectively.

During the first couple of years of college, I ran with what were then called "beboppers," with jazz musicians, in the middle fifties.

DM: Did you enjoy music?

MM: No, I didn't. I got very little out of music. It wasn't until later that I was able to get it. I listened to a lot of classical music and enjoyed it. I like Beethoven and Mozart most.

I ran with the beboppers, going to all their jam sessions and nightclub engagements and not really hearing their music until I had been listening to it for more than a year. I was doing it for the drugs and excitement and because you stayed up all night and slept all day. Then, one day, somebody was playing a record by Thelonious Monk. And I heard that. Then I heard Bud Powell and then I could hear it all. By that time, I was headed somewhere else.

DM: What did you hear in Thelonious Monk?

MM: A very exotic, highly structured, mysterious, emotional occasion. Elegance. Elegance of the intellect and the body moving in tune with the elements. Because you have to, you have to move. Move your hands around.

I found Monk and then, I think, I found Powell and then Gerry Mulligan and who was the young trumpet player with Mulligan . . .?

DM: Chet Baker.

MM: Chet Baker, Anita O'Day, Charlie Parker. I went through all of those: Gillespie, Parker, *Salt Peanuts*, *A Night in Tunisia, Ornithology, How High the Moon* . . . and a whole host of people I've almost forgotten. I listened to the music for a year before touching it. Before it even got through my skin.

DM: When did you get to San Francisco?

MM: 1954. I took Robert Duncan's poetry workshop, and I was handing in sonnets to Robert. Robert was astounded that a person who was so interested in poetry would hand in sonnets and villanelles. He kept trying to get me to write free verse, and I wasn't mature enough to explain to him that I had already been through it. Yet what I was doing interested him.

I think at first we were amazed with each other. I was amazed by his clarity of perception and his ability to express himself and to be concise. I had been through free verse, completely through free verse, and was experimenting with the very traditional forms like the sestina, the classical Petrarchan sonnet, and so on. Robert couldn't figure out why I was doing this, because he thought this kind of thing was a dead horse. For me, it was the final grounding in what I wanted to know before I split those forms completely.

We wrote poems every week and Robert would be slightly dismayed at my sonnets. It was a very interesting confluence. Then I became personal friends with Robert and with Jess. They offered an opening to the possibilities that I was searching for.

DM: Was he a good teacher?

MM: Fantastic. It was one of the most brilliant things that ever happened in my life. To have Robert stand at the blackboard and speak for two or three hours about a line of poetry, or a word, or a poem, or whatever came into his mind in relationship to his own work, or to the work that other people were bringing in. I believe in the cliché that poetry or painting can't be taught, but I was also present at the exception to the rule which makes the rule which was Robert's class.

DM: When did you start publishing?

MM: The next thing that happened was that I met Jonathan Williams and he offered to do my first book, *Passage*. It started out as a great stack of poems, but I kept editing them down. There was no size restriction. I imposed that restriction on myself.

I knew when I wrote those two villanelles for Roethke that meter and genre held no more interest for me. I had satisfied the desire to handle genre.

In looking at a sonnet you have to realize that you have an idea, a resolution of the idea, and a couplet to cap it. It makes you aware of the intellective process in writing the poem. Besides merely saying: I have a girl; it's spring; I got fucked; I didn't get fucked; the water is great; look, there's an animal ... I mean, it makes you realize that you have relationships other than those and you are forced to look at the structure of ideas behind a poem. A poem can't interest me very much unless it is both intellective and emotional.

All that was going through my head. It was like what was happening with the abstract expressionists at that time. They were learning to write their biographies in the movements of their body on a canvas. Whether this painting is looked at in two hundred or three hundred years was not of interest to me. What was of interest to me, although I couldn't formulate it until years later, was the fact that it was a spiritual occasion that I could believe in. And it was alive and brilliant while I looked at it. I was very much taken with that concept, and that's influenced me enormously. I still see things in those terms. I see rock and roll as a spiritual occasion. I saw the assemblage movement as being a spiritual occasion. I see the new earthwork sculpture as being a spiritual occasion. I saw Ginsberg as a spiritual occasion. The beat generation thing as being a spiritual occasion; the San Francisco renaissance as being a spiritual occasion. I feel as if I am a string and these spiritual occasions are beads or pearls that pass over me in much the same way that a complex molecule, RNA, slides across the ribosome to create protein. It's as if I am a string that the pearls, or ribosomes, of events pass over and from this I form the protein of my being around it.

If we are, in a sense, genetically indestructible until we are brought to our termination, I think it's reasonable that, rather than starting with a predisposed philosophy or cosmology, we allow it to form itself around us. I also have the feeling that everything grows. My relationships to things grow. Oh, there are dead spaces. There are the knots on a necklace between the pearls. I also look forward to the knots.

I think a lot of us tend to exist in static situations —very much to our loss. Some can exist statically because of drugs. They can exist statically because of the situation dealt to them. By luck, you fall upon certain concepts. You can also form a feedback of intellectivity or emotionality or physical being and throw it out and bring back more with it.

DM: Your many references to chemical procedures come from what revelation?

MM: In the last year I read a book called, *The Anatomy of the Cell,* by Björn Afzelius. He is a Swedish electromicroscopist. Although I had read quite a bit about genetic structure, it wasn't until I read this book that I totally changed my relationship to the material that we are made of—to our protoplasm. I realized that my picture of it was highly simplified. Even with a layman's understanding of contemporary microbiology, I still didn't have a picture of the complexity of the events that we are. I was still buying the idea we were given in high school that the cell is a kind of bag. I realized the complex structure within the bag, but I didn't realize that the structure within the bag *creates* the bag. Topologically, the inside of the cell is as complex a structure as we can conceive of. Any given cell. There are three trillion cells in each of us.

MM: I think your idea of, what did you say, rearranging the skin web is probably exactly where it's at.

DM: I think that's what it is. It has to do with facing a series of crises of *self-image*, self-perception, realizing the depth of the *selfless* forms.

MM: It happened when I wrote "Fleas."

DM: Some of which were in *Caterpillar: 8/9*?

MM: Yes. Those were the first nine. There are 250 of them. They are spontaneous and unrewritten. They're all in rhyme and average about twenty lines each. They are childhood memories. They are an obsession like Billy the Kid and Jean Harlow were obsessions. The idea of doing *Fleas* became an obsession and when I finished them and reread them, I found that I had awakened many of the more complex responses.

In other words, when I look at that chair I remember the chairs I've seen in my childhood which were out of mind before.

I became interested in the topology of how our mind works and about two-thirds of the way through writing, I discovered how information is stored hologramistically in the brain. In other words, in multitudinous sources, overlapping, instead of one, and it was precisely what was going on in me.

Everything overlaps everything else and lights it up. It isn't stored according to our ideas of rationality. It's stored on an organic basis and everything overlaps everything, and as one memory is lit, it lights the corner of another memory. If you light up another memory near it, it will light up a memory that was unsuspected. Then that lights the corner of another memory and you light up another one near it and it lights up the one in between.

The new sciences of microbiology have a very small relationship to the sciences that precede them. Böehme said that the universe we live in is the result of the friction of the celestial-bliss universe rubbing against the black fires—which I find as believable as atoms and molecules.

I think we have to believe everything that's reasonable to us. Boehme's concept of our existence is as spiritually true, or truer, than atoms and molecules.

In John Lilly's book *The Mind of the Dolphin,* he goes to great length about how little we know. And how much of mental health is accepting the things

that come from beyond limitations. Just accepting
them. I think that the more that happens to me that
I can take, per se, the happier I am. When you're
young and specters appear before you, you learn very
quickly to either not see specters anymore, or to accept the fact that specters appear. I accept.

DM: We often deny what we may be afraid of. The
unknown is often a fearful connation and becomes
an obstacle . . . There are aspects of the unknown
that provoke fear and we can face fear a lot of times
by rejecting it.

MM: Byron was afraid he would never die.

DM: So much of it is coming to accept whatever
happens, being able to cope with it without much
expectation.

MM: I think the most exciting thing that's happened
to me is the ability to think. When I say "think," it's
nothing so heavy. It's just that I will imagine I'm at
a Mexican temple in the year 1450 when it's being
inaugurated. Forty thousand people are being sacri-
ficed. Then I'll envision the scene and I'll skip from
there to another thought to another thought to
another thought, so that I can't . . . it's very difficult
for me to be bored anymore.

I saw Kerouac the day after he died.

DM: You did?

MM: Yes. I woke up in the morning and he was flying through blackness and it was great. And I yelled
at him: "Hey, hey!"

DM: And what did he say?

MM: He didn't say anything. I wrote a poem in my
mind. I didn't have my pen but I wrote down what
I could remember.

DM: Kerouac was important to you, wasn't he?

MM: Yes, absolutely. I think with Kerouac the most
important thing was that I don't agree with Kerouac
about very much. Yet I loved his writing. He is so
graphic and concrete that I experience what he ex-

perienced—even though it is totally foreign to me. And it knocks me out to know what he felt and what he saw. So that, in a sense, he is like a real paragon. If there were five hundred men like this that you could follow, you would really be in great shape. If you could see out of five hundred sets of eyes besides your own and smell through five hundred noses . . . I am willing to do it, if anybody will present it for me. I just read a book called *The Way of All Flesh* by Samuel Butler. It was of equal importance to me as the book on microbiology. I mean, to see into Victorian society and to see into the interior of the cell are two really great sights.

2

DM: When did you start writing plays?
MM: 1959. I finished the first one then. The first one was called *The Raptors*. Then I did a play called *The Blossom*. *The Feast* was next, a play in beast language.
DM: Could you explain the formulation of beast language?
MM: There was no evolution. The idea of *The Feast* sprang into my head, went off light a light bulb over my head—like in the cartoons. Flash, flash, flash! And I saw the whole play and I started to write it down in beast language with thirteen characters drinking black wine and eating loaves of French

bread. Then I said, this is ridiculous! And I started writing what I imagined I should do. I wrote a great deal but had to throw it all away and go back to what I originally saw, what first flashed over my head. That was the only beast language I wrote until three or four years later when I felt a ball of silence within myself—and inside of that ball was beast language. It was a source of pleasure, entertainment, and amusement and a great deal of concentration not to lose it. I knew there would be a hundred poems to write down as I heard them.

DM: We were talking earlier about the form, the contour of your work.

MM: I see what I'm doing as pulling out possibilities within myself. As a possibility opens itself, I create it. It isn't anything that wasn't already there. I can see the possibilities now.

DM: All these events hinge upon a moment, the available perception, your disposal toward the moment. As a spectator to your work, as the audience, I can sense from your work a kind of pattern of development.

MM: A lot of that has to do with my editing. A lot of it is self-acceptance. Like in *Hymns to St. Geryon,* I decided I should be what is represented there. In *The New Book/A Book of Torture,* I decided I should be what is represented there. Each one is like a very narrow vibration of what I am doing at a given time—what I felt was the most appropriate vibration.

There will be a lot of poems in my book that Grove is publishing right now, the book called *Star,* that are very much like the unpublished poems I was writing in 1955, 1956, and 1957, but I couldn't accept them then.

The beat thing was over the horizon. American culture creates these great slots and pigeonholes.

JS: And the San Francisco renaissance was yours?

MM: No.

JS: I mean, it was the one they put you in.

MM: Yes, I guess so. I highly disregard all that slot making. It looks like in the seventies all the slots are going to come down. I don't think we have to stand for the slots now. I think enough people have been slotted and pigeonholed. I think the audience can be depropagandized.

For one thing, everybody is going to be getting tired of the word "ecological," yet the ecological thrust is bringing people together. I recently wrote a poem beginning with two lines of a poem by Larry Eigner. I rediscovered Eigner's poems after not having paid close attention to him for a number of years. I got his *Another Time in Fragments* and began a poem with two lines of his and sent it to him along with my Rector poem. He responded with an article he had written on ecology and a three-page letter on thermal pollution.

JS: Has ecology been a long-time concern with you, or does the vocabulary and concern come late?

MM: I met Sterling Bunnell in 1957 and before that I thought in terms of biology or natural history or physiology or morphology. Sterling introduced the concept of ecology to me. So I would say it was a concern since 1957. Since then Sterling became and remained one of my best friends.

JS: You were in a play of Duncan's in the early fifties?

MM: Yes, I had one line.

JS: It must have been a good one. What was the line?

MM: I can't remember. The play was *Faust Foutu*.

JS: Did that kind of predate your interest or begin your interest in drama?

MM: Actually the performance of Robert's play was a reading of it. The play should be performed because it is a very important play. As far as I know it hasn't been given a public performance and I would

like to show it to John Lion of the Magic Theater to
see if it is possible.

I found the beginnings of a play in a 1956 notebook. I was grasping for a play, but was only able to
write dialogue. I wasn't able to carry the images of
the persons in my head as I was writing. Only their
voices. So it was unsuccessful.

It must have been about 1958 when Artaud's *The
Theater And Its Double* came out. I was convinced
by Artaud that texts were needed for the theater and
that it would be the poets who would write these
texts. I was inflamed with his idea of theater, and
the theater of cruelty. I've never been interested in
absurdism, aside from the theatrical possibilities of
it. But on reading Artaud, I looked at the poems that
I was writing and I thought that the poems were
voice notations. (These would be many of the poems
in *The New Book/A Book of Torture*.) I said, "Ah,
this voice notation can be adapted to theater! And
then I wrote *The Blossom*, a play about Billy the
Kid. Billy the Kid and the other participants in the
Lincoln County War in New Mexico in eternity together, unaware of their death and former relationships. They speak as if they are mobile and motile
sculptures in eternity.

JS: Has it been performed?

MM: Yes. It's been performed several times. It was
first performed about a year or two after it was
written. It was done at the Poets Theater in New
York by Diane Di Prima and Alan Marlowe with sets
by George Herms. I wasn't able to see it but I saw a
few minutes of film footage and it looked beautiful.
They did it together with an Artaud tape of *Let Us
Be Done with the Judgment of God*, the tape of his
voice done for Radiodiffusion Française. It had gotten
into the hands of Ginsberg and myself. *The Blossom*
was performed as a double bill with Artaud reading.

Then it was done at the University of Wisconsin by

Robert Cordier. They brought me in to give a poetry reading and to see the performance. The department had OK'd the production of the play, but when I got there they said: "No, no performance." They'd seen the rehearsals. "We won't allow this to run!" So two professors threatened to quit and one performance of the play was allowed. The public couldn't be let in— just people who happened to be wandering by. However, the auditorium was packed. A lot of people had heard about it. Cordier owned a film company and flew in people to film it and the university said: "if you film it we will kick the students out for participating in the filming." And I said: "Stop. Forget it." The snow was four feet deep outside. So, I guess, that was my first taste of censorship.

The Blossom was done again at the Straight Theater in San Francisco about two years ago. It was coupled with a mime drama of Artaud's.

DM: Did seeing one of your plays acted in any way affect the writing of the next play?

MM: Absolutely. When *The Cherub* was done here by the Magic Theater . . . I wrote *The Cherub* after I got back from London. After fourteen or fifteen busts of *The Beard,* I said "fuck the theater," and I wrote a novel. When I got back from the London performances of *The Beard,* where I received massive rave reviews, I felt very joyful about the theater and I wrote a couple of comic plays out of a feeling of happiness—and because the images were there within me to be developed. Actually, they just unfolded themselves from the start. John Lion asked me for a play to do at the Magic Theater and we did *The Cherub.* And when I saw *The Cherub* I was very pleased to see this play in existence, and I wrote ten more plays in the same genre. And I called the plays, eleven plays, *Gargoyle Cartoons.* You saw them, didn't you?

JS: Yes, I saw three of them.

MM: Well, they are all alike, and they are all totally different.

JS: Will they all be done eventually?

MM: The idea is that they are like Noh drama. Noh dramas comprise several plays. The body of *Gargoyle Cartoons* is eleven plays. The director can choose three, four, or five plays depending on his temper, upon circumstances. He can string them together, like: *Wolf Tooth, A Piece of Jade,* and *A Piece of Thistle Down.* He can make a sculpture out of a theatrical event with any group of plays he chooses.

JS: I saw things going on in the lobby prior to the beginning of the plays. Was that of your making also?

MM: I believe in the total extension of mise-en-scène. Recently I have written a play that totally breaks the stage space. I like to have the play set as meat on a shelf in space with lights and music so that they are sculptural. They actually have the three-dimensionality of meat presenting an image to you. For instance, *The Beard* is Billy the Kid and Jean Harlow in blue velvet. It's an image. Spider Rabbit is an image. The Two Meat Balls, the two balls of fur discussing the nature of reality, are image. The images are there and they unfold. The image is three-dimensional in my head. I can hear, see, smell, taste, touch it. When I conceive of that image it begins to unfold and it unfolds as a gargoyle cartoon.

It's an image of meat. A meat-sculptural concept which requires that I have it happen in my head. In 1955 or 1956, the only thing that was happening was literary. Voices in my head. The way you write a villanelle. You write a villanelle because there is a metrical voice in your head that you are pursuing. You demand it to rhyme in a certain pattern. But that's a voice, it's not dimensional.

Probably the very reason Robert was upset with traditional forms of poetry is that they are not dimensional. They can be, and it might be very inter-esting to make them dimensional again—as they were for Shelley or Keats. In contemporary terms, it's very hard to give any tactility to an inherited structured form. You want to get out there and stretch and push, and you want to give the imagery actuality, credibil-ity, and vitality. You know, Olson brought in the idea that you do it with a thrust of energy onto a field. This is an interesting concept.

JS: When we walked into the theater that night, there was a chick on a bed with a guy and on another side there was a guy doing yoga in a glass case, and on the other was a chick playing harp . . .

MM: And a guy in boxer's trunks skipping rope?

JS: Right. Were those pieces yours?

MM: And it was full of fog? And somebody was bar-b-queing meat and serving it to a couple at a table. The idea was mine. As mise-en-scène extending into the theater and connecting with the plays.

JS: I thought they were the fourth gargoyle cartoon.

MM: No, they weren't. Although in a sense they were. It was all done by a girl named Evalyn Stanley. I told her what kind of feeling I wanted in the lobby and everything that was there was hers. I may have said: "Somebody cooking meat." I didn't think of a boxer, I didn't think of a yogi in a glass case, but I said I wanted it full of fog and very bizarre happenings that were in context with the plays. So she arranged the whole thing. We were very fortunate in a costumer also. Besides the director and the actors. The cos-tumer and set designer were brilliant.

JS: It was a great way to get into the play.

MM: People became so hung up in the lobby that they would walk into one of the cartoons late 'cause they thought they were seeing the play.

JS: I spoke to people who thought we were, in fact, in the play.

MM: Yes. That's the way it should be. For instance,

when we did *The Beard* here, on the opening night
I had girls in strange costumes with whips and
masks, lead the audience to their seats. And there was
a show of George Herms's pieces in the lobby. I was
trying to extend the mise-en-scène as much as possible. There was a word on each seat that related
directly to the play. When you took your seat there
was a strip of paper on it printed in very very large
letters. It would say "silk" or "rock" or "boot" or
"pantie" or "blue" or "velvet" or "mark" or "tooth."
The audience would sit holding that piece of paper
they picked off their seat. Words that were repeated
in the play. The mise-en-scène can feed back on the
play.

In the play Billy the Kid would say: "There is
nothing here but blue velvet." One person is holding
"blue," and another person is holding "velvet."

I like the almost paleolithic quality of having a
stage, the very ancient idea of having a stage as a
shelf. The ritual of contemporary psychological
theater is that you walk in and confront the shelf. I
prefer the shelf to be confronted as a pedestal. The
total environment should be an entertainment—
which also relieves the play of the burden of entertainment. The play obviously should entertain, but
the play can also contain ideas. The mise-en-scène
can also contain ideas.

JS: The Living Theater has its own ideas about the
show confronting you.

MM: When the Living Theater breaks the stage space
and comes down into the audience I don't feel it is
so much a Pirandellian extrusion of the stage toward
me—I feel it's an actual extension of the stage up
and down the aisles. For instance, in their *Antigone,*
when the actors writhe up the aisles, I feel that they
are carrying the stage with them. This is a matter of
their presence more than anything else. I feel that
the stage is putting out tentacles to engulf me. I

don't feel that someone has come off the stage to break the reality of the rite.

I conceive of the play as being like a cell. It has its organelles, its ribosomes, and its DNA and RNA, and a good enactment of it is harmonically and biochemically in balance. You see this go wrong very easily when a director will allow an actor to take over a part for a laugh or a burst of applause.

Both actor and playwright have to create a living entity that gives rise and allows the spontaneous burst of applause, the laugh. So they are in balance with one another and create their universe around it. The sculptures of the persons within it are like the movements within a cell.

JS: In that first play, the one with the little guy and the three pandas and the three naked girls and the giant frog . . .

MM: That's called *The Pansy.*

JS: . . . so much of that was involved with blocking . . . and with my experience in the theater, blocking was on the shoulders of the director, not the playwright. I am wondering how much of that blocking you were responsible for and how much the director was responsible for. There is not a great deal of dialogue. A great deal of it is involved with the dance.

MM: John and I happened to be very much in agreement on many levels. I went to as many rehearsals as I could and approved of everything. I generally approve of what John does. I think *The Gargoyle Cartoons* are director's plays. Among other things, they allow extreme possibilities for the director. I think I can write a director's play because I'm sure enough of what is going on, on the stage. I think it will transmit itself with a great deal of accuracy to the director, and he will enjoy allowing it to manifest itself.

The other really interesting thing in drama is that it happens in your head in three dimensions—with

real imagined meat doing it, and then when it's actually performed with a real flesh body, it's so different,
and so much more real than when it happened in
your head. It takes on so many complexities of the
actor's temperament, of his stature, of his being,
and that is when it really gets interesting. That's
what stimulates you to go on in the theater.

JS: Spider Rabbit is black . . .

MM: I had not intended Spider Rabbit to be black.
As a matter of fact, I didn't want any racial overtones in the play. And I thought until the end that we
were going to have Chris do it in whiteface. We tried
it in whiteface and we said: "Oh, man, take it off!"
I am not aware of any racial overtones in it. We are
planning to do *The Beard* with a black Billy the
Kid, probably Chris. This will be interesting. I'd like
to see an all-black *The Beard*. I'd like to change
them to Mae West and W. C. Fields, or change them
to Mata Hari and the Heap. I'd like to have them
wear derbies with little halos on a stick over their
heads. Rip Torn would like that.

DM: Whatever happened with your confrontations
with censorship in Los Angeles?

MM: It's still being passed around the courts. Here is
an interesting book. I have a new publisher . . . the
State of California. This has almost a complete text
of *The Beard*. The state illustrated it for me and
added two hundred pages of commentary to it.

JS: Whose commentary?

MM: State senators, finks, canaries, musk turtles,
karmic debility cases.

DM: I hope you are well protected by good lawyers
and good vibrations . . .

MM: What's happening in LA is that I was convicted
of disturbing the peace. I wasn't convicted of ob-
scenity. I'm being sued for a half of a million dollars
and *The Beard* is being tried for fourteen arrests
on, I think, eighteen counts. Something like that.

They just arrested *The Beard* in Vancouver. Fortunately, the cast are being protected by the Canadian Civil Liberties Union. Again, it got very good reviews —as good as the reviews in London.

3

MM: What I am most concerned with now is the river within ourselves. The biological energy of ourselves is extrusions or tentacles of the universe of meat. The universe of life covering the entire planet. Let's say life is four billion years old—it might be older—from the first complex particles of a certain type of material joined together in strings and then coiling and encapsuling themselves. The next biggest step for them is to become links, to form a coating about themselves. Traditionally, you think of a cell as being an enclosed substance, like a bag or a sac. It's actually not that. It's created from the inside outward and it's highly complex topologically. From the first topological complexity becoming what we have come to call life until now—four billion years later.

If you could do as Spengler does. . . . He takes cultures and examines them side by side as if they were physical entities. If you can conceive of all life that has happened on this planet of which we are a highly complex extrusion, as a novelty of that body experience, and conceive of that body as unique, freed of time and space, and if you can conceive of it as a vast being . . . then you begin to conceive of yourself in relationship to the surge. It's not a systematic system. It is a systemless system, an expanding system, a system becoming complex as it stores rays of the sun. The rays of the sun furnish energy for this. It contains more and more of the energy and it grows more and more. You begin to see your relationship to it and you begin to see that there is a river, a surge, a source that is universal and that you partake of.

You are that thing, sensing and perceiving itself. You become dimly aware of the multiplicity of your sensations. You don't have five senses. Scientists say we have twenty-seven senses. You can't really conceive of this totality because you don't have an infinitude of senses. But we have more senses than we know we have. We have deeper relations to this universe. I think, for the first time, an awareness of it is coming to us.

Take Camus. There he is confronted with horror, anguish, nausea, forlornness, etc., because he conceived the meaninglessness of a man's gestures in a telephone booth. He's a member of a very heavy Catholic society that has come to think in traditional-humanistic terms. You are partaking of the same culture—a planetary culture that is interlinked. You participate in various degrees of types of wealth or poverty it offers you. Camus sees this and says: "Oh, my God, look at the utter meaninglessness."

When a man sees this and can't relate to the universe—not only to the universe but the universe of beings—his reaction is like nausea or horror. I think now we are freed to recognize the possibility against that. Against a background of pollution, horror and contamination, mass starvation, hallucination and psychosis.

JS: So the response then to four billion years of history is not nausea?

MM: I think it could be very well like joy if we could deal with our inner beings. If we realize that we are not one intelligence but many intelligences; that we are not one cell, but a congress of cells. If we can understand very clearly that we have developed two sets of emotions and psychology: the social emotions and the inner physiological emotions.

In a herd society (the traditional humanist herd society which really isn't humanitarian) we have developed a herd man, a *lumpen* man, whose motivations are exterior rather than inner-directed. It's possible for a man to blossom, yet very few men blossom.

DM: Do you think that the inner river directs us in some way?

MM: I think it's the important direction, but it's usually repressed by the social condition, by the snares and mazes and entrapments of the priest-centered society—as well as the graph of values that's made for you.

JS: There are people that would say that we could acknowledge the flow as being your history of life, but that acknowledgment of it doesn't bring to us any direction at all.

MM: Yes, but people always want solutions.

JS: No, direction.

MM: Let me skip from that for a minute and maybe you will see. Everybody wants a solution instead of realizing that the universe is a frontier, that the universe is a messiah for this whole total . . . this beatific complex meat structure that you are a tentacle, an aura, an extrusion, an experiencing of. They say instead, we want a solution, we want a utopia, we want bliss, we want progress, we want revolution, we want this, we want that. These are all simplistic solutions. It's like we are all trapped in *solutionism.* As one solution fails, another solution is tried. Everybody wants a solution. When they realize the defeat of a solution they split as rapidly as they can to another solution to rid themselves of any anxiety.

It has to be seen very clearly that biological creatures do not exist with solutions. Biological creatures exist through motility and growth and the more complex constellations of memory, intuition, and perceptions of their sensorium. So you constantly destroy and re-create. You don't have a revolution to solve everything. Each creature is in a state of revolt, each intellective creature. Each creature that is able to feel with his meat . . . man or snake or wolf or rosebush . . . is in revolt, whether its revolt is its growth or whether the revolt is the deliberate making, the deliberate extrusion, the feedback loops to bring them what they want. To bring them what they want through manipulation of circumstances. But never technologically and not mechanistically.

JS: Those would be our answers, though.

MM: If the organism exists with problems then the organism also exists with possibilities for solutions. All I am saying is we can grant recognition of that river within us which, in mixed vocabulary, could be the Hindu "We are all one," but it would seem that that doesn't lend any solution. "We are all one" is too easy. "I am many" is more where it's at. I am happy when my manys agree.

I am many is where it is at. I am a heart, I am three trillion cells, I am a lung, I am many neuronal centers; I am an obvious sensorium that sights, tastes, touches, smells, that I can verbalize and symbolize about—I am twenty-two other senses that are less easy to verbalize or symbolize about, several of which are totally unconscious and don't register on the part of the brain that I constantly recognize.

The manys of me must agree and must find what

I call an intellectivity to commune with, free of desire for solutions or progress. We must look for Mammalian betterment.

Our genes are one-and-a-half million years old. We spent one-and-a-half million years minus twenty thousand years developing at one thing and spent the last twenty thousand years selectively breeding to become something else . . . and developing a tradition that's not what the biological preparation was for. He evolved as a rare creature. We are no longer a rare creature. We evolved as a social animal and we are becoming a herd animal; or, gregarious as opposed to the social animal.

JS: I'm wondering, with such an extreme and powerful overview, if you could draw it down to specifics that are meaningful within the deliberate confines of one's rational thought.

MM: I don't think one man can do it—unless that one man is a great visionary. I don't think one man can do it. Man is a rare animal, but man is also a social animal. I don't think one man would find it. It's again like wanting a messiah, a leader . . . It's going to have to be a pool of intellective, multiple intelligences, to conceive of creative betterment, or find what we are "naturally" biologically and bring the possibilities of that into play.

We are very unhealthy. We were much healthier thirty thousand years ago. We were much more intelligent thirty thousand years ago. Thirty thousand years ago we had larger brains, and more possibilities of constellative configurations. We probably were more perceptive thirty thousand years ago. There's been a great deal of selective breeding since the domestication of animals and cultivation of plants. We have developed a new type of man in a very brief time. We've done it the same way that you can develop new types of dogs. You can have Chihuahua, you can have a Great Dane, you can have a Malamute, from one stock. We have opted for one of the possibilities of our stock and it seems to be highly unsatisfactory.

On the other hand, we can't romanticize the talk about Tarzan and Jane, or the noble savage, because that is a manifest absurdity. I mean, that's another kind of kitsch. No one man, or individual, or small group of individuals can conceive of the situation.

JS: Let's say at the beginning of Western history, at the time of the Academy, one small group of men supposedly had a vision of . . .

MM: Are you talking of Plato and Socrates?

JS: Say that the Platonic Academy is an idea . . .

MM: That was merely the development of the tradition that was already in existence.

JS: It was more than that, it was the bringing together . . .

MM: I love Plato. Not only do I enjoy reading him, but I consider *The Symposium* to be a truly great absurdist drama when it is performed—and not read. I don't think Plato could have been a playwright in that day when the Greek theater was so different from his ideas. What he did was to write closet comedies that are very beautiful.

JS: The notion of the Academy that I meant was that it absorbed the countryside . . . they absorbed the folklore and history and they wrung it through a kind of strainer and out came Western civilization as we know it.

MM: No. Look at what was happening at exactly the same time. Out of the East comes a mystery cult. From the population centers of the East, probably Egypt . . .

JS: Plato visited Egypt and was a disciple of Zoroaster, so he was in touch with the East . . .

MM: I'm thinking of the confluence. You are looking at the Academy as being the major origin of our humanist condition, but at this period there is a confluence. The mystery cults travel from the population centers of the East. The mystery cults are obviously a reaction to population density. They say you will be reborn, that you will be given rebirth within our community and that you will have immortality. The cult is evangelistic and these cults battle it out. Finally you have Mithraism which was the predominant mystery cult at the time of the conception of Christianity.

The Christians have destroyed practically all traces of Mithraism. We know very little about it. The Christians were the highly jealous winners of that battle of the cults. Christianity triumphed as a mystery cult. It was even more evangelistic than Mithraism. The whole society becomes a mystery cult and the mystery becomes totally exoteric, totally at the service of the traditional humanism, and it conjoins with the traditional humanism to become a servant of it—bringing with it all the shit to support the worst hypocrisies, the natural bloodthirsty drives, as well as the kind human temperament. These ideas comingle, conjoin, confluence, and here we are.

This is apparently not only true of the West. A similar thing happened throughout the entire world. We are joined in a tightly locked total surface planet culture. This is only one possibility among many possibilities. It happens to be the one we have arrived at. I don't see any elements in any civilization that weren't a contribution to where we are at now. You can find the Mayans destroying Mexico. They did a pretty good damn beginning of it before the Spaniards got there.

JS: When you mentioned that perhaps a group of men would have a vision powerful enough to use, I thought of the Platonic Academy. Things have been happening for the last four or five years where people have seemingly been calling for another Platonic Academy.

MM: It will have to be a mammalian one. It would be right if we could get a few eagles and bears and dolphins in there too, not to mention salmon, bison, and pandas.

I'd like to repeat something that's in *Meat Science Essays* because you brought up Plato. One of the Greek mottoes that they liked to live by was: "Moderation is best." Moderation is highest. One of the catchphrases of our acculturated traditional humanistic societies is also "moderation." I discovered that what we now mean by moderation and what the Greeks meant by moderation are two entirely different things.

The Greeks went to extremes. You get drunk and have belladonna in your wine and have a feast and everyone talks euphorically all night long and then, in the morning, you take your baths and go to the agora and to the marketplace and then to exercise. You go from the extreme of drunkenness to meditation to the body athletic. It was the development of both the body and the mind, the ability to sing, the possibility of being drunk and the possibility of soberness, yet we hypocritically, and antibiologically, give lip service to a different kind of moderation. Our moderation of today is like the moderation of the relative confinement of your possible activities. To be in your car, to drive it to work, to do a job, to come home, to have a drink, to go to bed, to go to work the next day.

The individual in his own idealism, which is propaganda, is blocked in his possibilities and the only possibilities that are open to him are the possibilities of checks and balances. Like, alcohol is OK— you can be excessive with alcohol because alcohol is traditionally inherent in this society. If you smoke grass then that gives you extra societal insights at this point. When grass becomes legal it will probably cease to do so. But at this time. it gives you extra societal insights, therefore it's a negative.

DM: The idea of moderation, doesn't it also arise from perhaps an instinct for a kind of balance?

MM: Yes, but the point I want to make is that the only balance you can achieve, that makes sense biologically is to go not to the extreme of freezing yourself to death or burning yourself to death, but to find a center, a balance, a true moderation. You have to go to many extremes to form a center that is the true balance. From this balance center you have to have extensions to conceive of what the possible frontiers are.

You must know what you can do. You have to experience what you can do. And then you must choose your moderation from the possibilities. You create your moderation. Today, your moderation is handed to you.

Sexuality is highly orthodox and it's rebelled against because of the intensity of the orthodoxy. The social unit is so orthodox that it seems inescapable. I mean, the family unit. The whole thing is not working. And won't work. It starts with a child. As a child learns to form what he sees into patterns, he's told specifically what the patterns are. He is propagandized as soon as he learns to organize sound.

A real biological moderation would be the result of a choice, i.e., I tried this and I tried that and I tried all of these other things, and I can do all of these other things, and I stand in relationship to all of these things.

Me, inner me, says I know what is happening. Nowadays, the inner me is smothered in favor of the social me. Social me is informed about the condition and if social me isn't propagandized by word alone, he is propagandized by example and by the stress of overpopulation. Everyone conforms more and more as the swirl becomes more and more psychotic.

DM: What are the alternatives for this society that you see as a poet?

MM: I think Blake is an extraordinary example. Blake was a man in revolt; he was constantly in revolt. He developed a system that constantly expanded. It was very vigorous because he very seldom took the time for self-examination or denial. He accepted the changes as his perceptions, intuitions, visions, and sensorium absorbed more and more. He expanded. He expanded as a rose plant would expand, or as any like creature in a natural habitat would expand; and, at the same time, he took a stand against all he didn't believe in. He didn't live in an ivory tower. That's what I'm saying. He didn't sit in a warfield in Vietnam with a copy of *Walden* in his back pocket and a flamethrower in his hand saying: "I'm really not here because I really believe in Walden."

DM: Blake had his treasure, he had his garden.

MM: Every man has his treasure. It's inside him. It's called meat.

DM: That's it.

MM: Most men are propagandized and negated by a structure that has become so all-encompassing that only a man born in the fortune of circumstance with certain intelligences is able to see some crack in the structure.

JS: The man who sees the cracks in the structure can still have his garden . . . can still have his inner peace.

MM: No. I don't think so. Not now. If you take a populist view and look back thirty or forty years, you could find the man out in the farm with a sense of meaningfulness. But now farms are factory farms. Chickens are raised by the tens of thousands in conditions that are unbelievable. And I guess 80 or 90 percent of our population is in major metropolitan

areas, so I don't think there is a possibility of it—
except in the most extraordinary conditions.
JS: Not in yours or my definition of the garden of
serenity, but perhaps these people have different
notions of it . . .
MM: There is no garden of serenity, there is no peace,
saving that you insulate yourself and lock the
doors . . .
JS: Or you watch TV.
MM: That's not peace. That's a jitterbug thing. It's
propaganda. It's a form of propaganda, a constant
barrage of propaganda informing you of all the kitsch
beliefs of the humanist tradition.
JS: TV is perhaps another man's garden of serenity
and meditation; a chapel of all the bullshit mysticism
for the last ten thousand years. The warden at Lom-
poc Prison puts the TV on in the morning and it
stays on all day. He says if it weren't for TV they
would have more riots.
MM: It's a baby-sitter.
JS: It takes care of people. It's a garden of serenity.
DM: How can you be serene when you can't see anything grow in your garden?
MM: It's a narcosis.
JS: Doesn't it take away the pain of life?
MM: I don't think it takes away the pain. I would
consider TV a pain-inflicting instrument. What actually happens psychologically when you watch TV is
that you get into a state of self-induced autohypnosis.
TV is a strong autohypnotic. You become fixated on
that screen which is projecting itself at you. Nothing
else registers on your reticular system, your neuronal
screen. The neuronal screen, the screen of your being, is meant to experience the universe, instead TV
fills it with the projection of shit images. It whites
out. I mean it whites your perceptions out. Sound
comes at you loud. The visual thing comes at you

very loud. As McLuhan points out, it appeals to your tactile sensorium as well. At least three areas of your sensorium are being hit at once. And it's all registering on that interior screen that's like a central source screen, or the central agency, for perception. All it does is white you out.

It fills you not with pleasurable influences but with painful influences: cowboys naked to the waist beating each other with chains. It's a mistake to equate the internalization of novelty with a desire for motility. Your body desires to move; your body desires activity, desires a frontier, so that your neuronal screen, actually your reticular system, the place where these images register, will be constantly active. You just lay there and it fills the screen. That screen was developed for an entirely different recognition pattern and perception pattern.

JS: I'm saying that the autohypnosis of TV is easily equated to meditation.

MM: No, because it's not filling enough to be equated to meditation. Meditation works in an entirely different way.

JS: Meditation is autohypnosis.

MM: There are several kinds of meditation. Let me give you two. One is the kind that is done in Subud. You move your arms and legs randomly in a darkened room with your eyes closed. You shout or sing or chant rhythmically at the same time. Try to think while you are doing that! It's impossible. Your screen is blank. Totally blank. And your screen being totally blank, you are getting a feedback of your own sensations. Purely physiological sensations. Totally organic sensations of your body with absolute imagelessness feeding back to you. You realize you are the universe. Afterwards you feel high. You really feel good. An hour of that is fantastically rewarding!

The other kind of meditation is much more complex. You do it through a series of studies and rejections and acceptances. You learn to empty the reticular system or your neuronal screen. Either one works. What I am saying is that TV is not emptying your screen, it is only filling it up enough to white it out. You're not getting any feedback. When it gets blank you get feedback. After watching TV, notice that you feel exhausted. You have been through the meat wringer. After meditation, either Subud-type meditation or Hindu Buddhist–type meditation, you feel invigorated. Sure those TV-watching people don't riot, they're too exhausted.

DM: I was interested in your relationship to Wilhelm Reich. What effect did his work have on you and where did it lead you to?
MM: Reich came like a bolt out of heaven for me. I found the muscular contractions and armoring he speaks of to be quite clearly within my own body. I tried to find a Reichian analyst. There wasn't one on the West Coast. I worked through experiments, exercising, automatic writing, and a lot of good friends and luck to find the armorings and to do what I could to eliminate them. I was in a state of extraordinary biological distress when I stumbled onto his work. I found it to be a great godsend, messiah-send—if the messiah is the universe.

Automatic writing is an extraordinarily helpful device if you just write what you want to write and know that nobody will ever see it.
DM: I remember at that time that you were also very much interested in Yeat's book *A Vision*.
MM: I was very much taken up with his concept of gyres. In the sense of gyre that you have the helix of the DNA molecule—although the DNA molecule is a crumpled gyre. You can see that the gyre represents an ever-expanding systemless system.
DM: The DNA molecule contains evidence of memory and history . . .

MM: The DNA molecule *is* the memory. It is the memory of the meat. Four billion years of memory telling you to be a mammal. Let me read you something here.

But desire to know and feel are not eased!
To feel the caves of body and the separate
physical tug of each desire is insanity. The key
is love
and yearning. The cold sea beasts
and mindless creatures are the holders of vastest
Philosophy.
We can never touch it.

We are blessed.

Praise to the surge of life that there is no answer
—and no question!

Genetics and memory

are the same

they are degrees of one

molecular unity.

Besides our body's being a genetic accretion of billions of years, it is the actual accretion of our physical contacts with our environments, our psychological contacts with our propaganda and our intuitions. It's the actual meat on your bones, the constellation of the perception and events, and, in addition, we have a storage center in which the events that we can symbolize and verbalize about are activated. We call it our cortex. There are other parts of the brain too, like that small part of the brain back there in the nasal area. In that area they have come to believe that memory is stored hologramistically. Memory isn't stored in one place but stored constellatively in many places within the mind. Memory multiplies and lights up the edges that the constellation overlaps. The electrical and chemical activity that goes on—several sources of it going simultaneously— are constantly interacting. This universe of cells is in constant action.

If we empty this screen then the experience is the universe. The body of the universe manifested in our body. If we allow the screen to be filled, then the screen is like the external reality vying with the inner reality. Biologically it's uncanny. If the existentialists were confronted with this they would have no answer—or they would want no answer. "How can this be? Where's God, why are we here? What is that man doing in the phone booth?"

Our bodies are like a multitude of fairy lands that all agreed to become you.

There's no doubt that there's a very high alchemy that we haven't touched yet. And that we have intuitions of in mūdras and gestures. A cell in the tip of your finger might be related to an atom in a star in another galaxy in a way we can't conceive of. The universe is an interweaving of such complexity that we are totally unable to conceive of it. You can imagine butterflies flying randomly through a shifting lattice. Can you imagine the multitudes of invisible presences surrounding it?

I think that what we've done is to choose the Faustian path in which we conceive of ourself as a tool or a mechanism. This choice is mirrored in technology. We conceive of our body as a tool or mechanism for the achievement of desires, rather than for the central being, the inner being, that creates and seeks in the outer and peers deeper into the inner.

We think of manipulating exterior reality and ourselves as tools, as functions of something we can't touch because it isn't there. It's an abstraction . . .
DM: The mysteries . . .
ANOTHER VOICE: You're in the ninth sphere . . .

Fall, 1969

List of Works by the Five Poets

Kenneth Rexroth

Poetry

"In What Hour." NY, 1940
"The Signature of All Things." New Directions, NY, 1949
"The Dragon and the Unicorn." New Directions, Norfolk, 1952
"In Defense of the Earth." New Directions, Norfolk, 1956
"The Collected Shorter Poems." New Directions, NY, 1966 (pb)
"The Collected Longer Poems." New Directions, NY, 1967
"The Heart's Garden, The Garden's Heart." Pym-Randall, Cambridge, 1967 (pb)

"Sky Sea Earth." Unicorn Press, Santa Barbara, 1970.
"New Poems." New Directions, NY, 1974.

Plays

"Beyond the Mountains." City Lights, SF, 1969 (pb)

Translations

"100 Poems from the Chinese." New Directions, NY, 1955 (pb)
"100 Poems from the Japanese." New Directions, NY, 1956 (pb)
"30 Spanish Poems of Love and Exile." City Lights, SF, 1959 (pb)
"Poems from 'The Greek Anthology." U. of Michigan Press, Ann Arbor, 1962 (pb)

"Love and the Turning Year: One Hundred More Poems from the Chinese." New Directions, NY, 1970.

"Love Is an Art of Time: One Hundred More Japanese Poems." New Directions, NY, 1971.

"The Orchid Boat: Women Poets of China [w/Ling Chung]." Herder and Herder/McGraw-Hill, NY, 1972.

Essays

"Bird in The Bush." New Directions, NY, 1959 (pb)

"Assays." New Directions, NY, 1961 (pb)

"The Alternative Society." Herder and Herder, NY, 1970

"American Poetry in the Twentieth Century." Herder and Herder, NY, 1971.

"With Eye and Ear." Herder and Herder, NY, 1972.

"The Elastic Retort: Essays in Literature and Ideas." Herder and Herder, NY, 1973.

"Communalism: From its Origins to the Twentieth Century." Continuum Books, NY, 1975.

Autobiography

"An Autobiographical Novel." Doubleday, NY, 1966; New Directions, NY, 1969 (pb)

William Everson (Brother Antoninus)

Poetry

"These Are the Ravens." Great West Publishing Co., San Leandro, 1935

"San Joaquin." Ward Ritchie Press, LA, 1939

"The Masculine Dead: Poems 1938–40." James Decker Press, Prairie City, 1942

"X War Elegies." Untide Press, Waldport, 1943

"The Waldport Poems." Untide Press, Waldport, 1944

"The Residual Years." New Directions, NY, 1948

"Triptych for the Living." Seraphim Press, Oakland, 1951
("Printed on the handpress and bound by William Everson at Maurin House, a Catholic Worker house of hospitality in Oakland, Califronia. 200 copies, of which less than 100 were issued, the remaining sheets destroyed." Kherdian: *Six Poets of the San Francisco Renaissance: Portraits & Checklists*, Gilgia Press, Fresno, 1967.)

"The Crooked Lines of God." U. of Detroit Press, Detroit, 1959

"The Hazards of Holiness: Poems 1957–60." Doubleday, NY, 1962

"The Poet Is Dead (A Memorial for Robinson Jeffers)." Auerhahn Press, SF, 1964

"Single Source: The Early Poems of William Everson (1939–40)." Oyez, Berkeley, 1966

"The Residual Years: Poems 1934–48." New Directions, NY, 1968 (pb)

"The Rose of Solitude." Doubleday, NY, 1968

"The City Does Not Die." Oyez, Berkeley, 1969

"A Canticle to the Waterbirds (with photographs by Allen Say)." Eizo, Berkeley, 1968.

"The Last Crusade." Oyez, Berkeley, 1969.

"Who Is She that Looketh Forth as the Morning?" Capricorn Press, Santa Barbara, 1972.

"Tendril in the Mesh." Cayucos Books, SF, 1973.

"The Black Hills." Didymus Press, SF, 1973.

"Man-Fate: The Swan Song of Brother Antoninus." New Directions, NY, 1974.

Essays

"Robinson Jeffers: Fragments of an Older Fury." Oyez, Berkeley, 1968

"Earth Poetry." Oyez, Berkeley, 1971.

Lawrence Ferlinghetti

Poetry

"Pictures of a Gone World." City Lights, SF, 1955 (pb)
"A Coney Island of the Mind." New Directions, Norfolk, 1958 (pb)
"Starting from San Francisco." New Directions, NY, 1961 (pb)
"The Secret Meaning of Things." New Directions, NY, 1968 (pb)
"Tyrannus Nix?" New Directions, NY, 1969 (pb)
"Back Roads to Far Towns." City Lights, SF, 1970 (pb)
"Love Is No Stone on the Moon." Arif Press, Berkeley, 1971.
"Back Roads to Far Places." New Directions, NY, 1971.

Plays

"Unfair Arguments with Existence." New Directions, NY, 1963 (pb)
"Routines." New Directions, NY, 1964 (pb)
"Mexican Night: A Travel Journal." New Directions, NY, 1970.

Novels

"Her." New Directions, NY, 1960 (pb)

Translations

"Jacques Prevert: Paroles." City Lights, SF, 1958

Lew Welch

Poetry

"Wobbly Rock." Auerhahn Press, SF, 1960

"Hermit Poems." 4 Seasons Foundation, SF, 1965

"On Out." Oyez, Berkeley, 1965; 1968 (pb)

"Courses." Dave Haselwood, SF, 1967; Cranium Press, SF, 1968 (pb)

"The Song Mt. Tamalpais Sings." Maya, SF, 1970

"Redwood Haiku and Other Poems." Cranium Press, SF, 1972.

"Ring of Bone: Collected Poems," 1950–1971 (Edited by Donald M. Allen). Grey Fox Press, Bolinas, 1972.

"Trip Trap: Haiku Along the Road from San Francisco to New York, 1959" (w/Jack Kerouac and Albert Saijo). Grey Fox Press, Bolinas, 1973.

Essays

"How I Work as a Poet and Other Essays" (Edited by Donald M. Allen). Grey Fox Press, Bolinas, 1973.

Michael McClure

Poetry

"Passage." Jargon, Big Sur, 1956

"Hymns to St. Geryon and Other Poems." Auerhahn Press, SF, 1959

"The New Book/A Book of Torture." Grove Press, NY, 1961 (pb)

"Dark Brown." Auerhahn Press, SF, 1961; Dave Haselwood, 1969 (pb)

"Ghost Tantras." Printed by the author, SF, 1964 (pb)

"Poisoned Wheat." Privately printed (Oyez), Berkeley, 1965; Coyote Press, 1966 (pb)

"Dark Brown and Hymns to St. Geryon." Cape Goliard, London, 1969

"Star (Poems 1964–70)." Grove Press, NY, 1970 (pb)

"The Book of Joanna." Sand Dollar, Berkeley, 1973.

"A Fist Full, 1956–1957." Sparrow: 16, January 1974. Black Sparrow Press, LA, 1974.

"Rare Angel (Writ With Raven's Blood)." Black Sparrow Press, LA, 1974.

"September Blackberries." New Directions, NY, 1974.

"Fleas, 189–195." Aloe Editions, NY, 1974.

Plays

"The Beard." Grove Press, NY, 1967 (pb)

"Little Odes and the Raptors." Black Sparrow Press, LA, 1969 (pb)

"The Mammals." Cranium Press, SF, 1972.

"Gargoyle Cartoons, or The Charbroiled Chinchilla." Delacorte Press, NY, 1971.

Essays

"Meat Science Essays." City Lights, SF, 1963 (pb)

Novels

"The Mad Cub." Bantam Books, NY, 1970 (pb)

"The Adept." Delacorte, NY, 1971

"Organism. Curriculum of the Soul" (#24), Canton, 1974.

"Freewheelin' Frank, Secretary of the Angels." Grove Press, NY, 1971.

Bookstores

Many of these books & pamphlets are not available at your local bookstore. The most realistic reason is that they are issued in small editions & circulate through an underground circuit of specialized bookstores. Here is a list of some of the shops that deal in modern poetry & writing. They can be of great assistance in locating both new & old materials.

Cold Mountain Press
4406 Duval
Austin, Texas 78751

City Lights
1562 Grant Avenue
San Francisco, Calif. 94133
(Publisher; catalog)

Gotham Book Mart & Gallery
41 West 47th Street
New York, N.Y. 10036
(Catalog)

Phoenix Book Shop
18 Cornelia Street
New York, N.Y. 10014
(Catalog; small-press distributor)

Sand Dollar Books
1205 Solano Avenue
Albany, California 94706

Serendipity Books
1790 Shattuck Avenue
Berkeley, Calif. 94709
(Catalog; small-press distributor)

Small Press Book Club
Box 1906
San Pedro, California 90733

Spring Church Book Company
Box 127
Scranton, Pennsylvania 15686

For addresses of magazines and publishers consult the annual directory put out by Dust Books, 5218 Scottwood Road, Paradise, Calif. 95969.

Printers

After compiling this list it became clear to me how well the poets in the Bay Area have been served by the printers. In the past two decades San Francisco has also been the place where the printer has produced some of the most consistently attractive books published in America. Hand-crafted work, usually involving type hand-set on special papers—meticulous, thoughtful work. The care they have lavished on the poet's art is truly remarkable and deserves a much richer history than this list.

Peter Bailey (East Wind)
Paul Beattie (M-C Press)
Wilder Bentley
Wallace Berman (Semina)
Clifford Burke (Cranium Press; Maya; Oyez)
The Colt Press
Joe Dunn (White Rabbit Press)
Henry Evans (Porpoise Press; Peregrine Press)
The Grabhorn Press
Don Gray (Two Windows Press)
Dave Haselwood (Auerhahn Press; Dave Haselwood Books)
Andrew Hoyem (Auerhahn Press; Grabhorn-Hoyem)
Graham Mackintosh (White Rabbit; Open Space; Oyez; Black Sparrow Press)
Bern Porter (Circle Books; Bern Porter Books)
The Print Workshop
Jack Staufacher (Greenwood Press)
Adrian Wilson
Noel Young (Black Sparrow Press; Christopher Books)

Courses

The last list is what Lew Welch might call a "course." I've put together a reading list of books available by men whose names were mentioned and discussed during the interviews. It makes a map of culture and you can use it as you like. Any of the roads lead ahead.

Anderson, Sherwood. "Short Stories." (ed. Geismar). Hill & Wang, NY, 1962 (pb)
———. "Winesburg, Ohio." Signet Books, NY, 1956 (pb)
———. "Letters." Kraus Reprints, NY, 1969
———. "Return to Winesburg" (ed White). U. of N. Carolina, Chapel Hill, 1967
———. "Story Teller's Story" (ed. White). U. of N. Carolina, Chapel Hill, 1968
———. "Tar: A Mid-West Childhood" (ed. White). U. of N. Carolina, Chapel Hill, 1969

(The last 3 titles are part of a series of Anderson's works offered in critical editions utilizing unpublished material from his manuscripts.)

Aragon, Louis. "Selected Writings." New Directions, Norfolks.

Artaud, Antonin. "Artaud Anthology" (ed. Hirschman). City Lights, SF, 1965 (pb)
———. "Theatre and Its Double" (tr. Richards). Grove Press, NY, 1958 (pb)
———. "Here Then the Question." Filthythumb Press, SF, 1968 (pb)
———. "Collected Works: Volume 1" (tr. Corti). Calder, London, 1968

———. "Oeuvres Complètes" (7 vols. French & European Publications, NY, 1956–57 (pb)

Auden, W. H. "Collected Longer Poetry." Random House, NY, 1969
———. "Collected Shorter Poems, 1927–57." Random House, NY, 1967
———. "Selected Poetry." Modern Library, NY, 1959
———. "Dyer's Hand." Vintage Books, NY, 1968 (pb)

Baudelaire, Charles. "Selected Flowers of Evil" (tr. Jackson & Mathews). New Directions, NY, 1958 (pb)
———. "Flowers of Evil" (tr. Dillon & Millay). Washington Square, NY, 1963 (pb)
———. "20 Prose Poems" (tr. Hamburger). Grossman, NY, 1968 (pb)
———. "Paris Spleen" (tr. Varese). New Directions, NY, 1969 (pb)

Blake, William. "Selected Poetry" (ed. Todd). Dell, NY, 1960. (pb)
———. "Complete Writings" (ed. Keynes). OUP, NY, 1966 (pb)
———. "Poetry and Prose" (ed. Erdman). Doubleday, NY, 1965
———. "Marriage of Heaven & Hell." U. of Miami, Coral Gables, 1968 (pb)
———. "The Book of Urizen." U. of Miami, Coral Gables, 1969 (pb)
(The last 2 titles are black and white photo-facsimiles of the original Blake text-engravings.)

———. "Portable William Blake" (ed. Kazin). Viking, NY, 1946 (pb)

Burns, Robert. "Complete Poetical Works" (Riverside ed.). Houghton Mifflin, NY.
———. "Poems and Songs" (ed. Kingsley). Dutton Everyman, NY, 1958
———. "Selected Poems" (ed. Fraser). Barnes & Noble, NY, 1960 (pb)
———. "Selected Poetry and Prose" (ed. Thornton). Houghton Mifflin, NY, 1966 (pb)

Burroughs, William. "Junkie." Ace, NY, 1953 (pb)
———. "Naked Lunch." Grove Press, NY, 1962, (pb)

240

——. "Yage Letters" (w/Allen Ginsberg). City Lights, SF, 1963 (pb)

——. "Nova Express." Grove, NY, 1964 (pb)

——. "The Soft Machine." Grove, NY, 1966 (pb)

——. "Ticket That Exploded." Grove, NY, 1967 (pb)

——. "Minutes to Go" (w/Beiles, Corso & Gysin). Beach Books, SF, 1968 (pb)

——. "So who Owns Death TV?" Beach Books, SF. (pb)

Cendrars, Blaise. "Selected Writings" (ed. Albert). New Directions, NY. (pb)

Chaucer, Goeffrey. "Canterbury Tales" (tr. Coghill). Penguin, 1952 (pb)

——. "Chaucer" (ed. Coxe). Dell, NY, 1963 (pb)

——. "Complete Works" (ed. Skeats). OUP, NY, 1933

——. "Troilus and Cresyde" (ed. Cooke). Vintage, NY, 1959 (pb)

Chomsky, Noam. "American Power and the New Mandarins." Vintage, NY, 1969 (pb)

——. "Aspects of the Theory of Syntax." MIT, Cambridge, 1965 (pb)

——. "Language and Mind" (text). Harcourt, Brace & World, NY, 1968 (pb)

Cocteau, Jean. "5 Plays." Hill & Wang, NY, 1961 (pb)

——. "Difficulty of Being" (tr. Howard). Coward-McCann, NY, 1967

——. "Holy Terrors" (tr. Lehmann). New Directions, NY, 1966 (pb)

——. "Imposter." Citadel, NY, 1966 (pb)

——. "The Infernal Machine and Other Plays." New Directions, NY, 1963 (pb)

——. "Journals of" (tr. Fowlie). Indiana U. Press, Bloomington, 1964 (pb)

——. "Opium: Diary of a Cure" (tr. Crosland & Reid). Hillary, NY, 1957

——. "Screenplays" (tr. Martin-Spery). Orion/Grossman, NY, 1969

——. "Two Screenplays" (tr. Martin-Spery). Penguin, NY, 1969 (pb)

Cohen, Leonard. "Beautiful Losers." Viking, NY, 1969 (pb)

——. "Favorite Game." Viking, NY, 1963

――――. "Selected Poems." Viking, NY, 1968 (pb)

――――. "Songs of Leonard Cohen." Collier, NY, 1969 (pb)

Crane, Hart. "Complete Poems and Selected Letters and Prose" (ed. Weber). Anchor, NY, 1966 (pb)

――――. "Letters of" (ed. Weber). U. of California Press, Berkeley, 1952 (pb)

Creeley, Robert. "Charm: Early and Uncollected Poems." 4 Seasons, SF, 1968 (pb)

――――. "For Love, Poems 1950–60." Scribner, NY, 1962 (pb)

――――. "The Gold Diggers" (stories). Scribner, NY, 1965 (pb)

――――. "Island" (a novel). Scribner, NY, 1963 (pb)

――――. "Pieces." Scribner, NY, 1969 (pb)

――――. "Words." Scribner, NY, 1967 (pb)

――――. "Quick Graph" (essays). 4 Seasons, SF, 1970 (pb)

――――, ed. *The Black Mountain Review, 1–7* (reprint). AMS, NY, 1969

Cummings, E. E. "Selection of Poems." Harvest, NY. (pb)

――――. "The Enormous Room." Modern Library, NY, 1934

――――. "i: Six non-lectures." Athenenum, NY, 1962 (pb)

――――. "Poems: 1923–54." Harcourt, Brace & World, NY, 1954

Dickinson, Emily. "Complete Poems of" (ed. Johnson). Little, Brown, Boston, 1960 (The definitive collection.)

――――. "Letters of" (ed. Todd). Harper & Bros, 1931

――――. "Selected Poems." Modern Library, NY, 1948

――――. "Selected Poems and Letters" (ed. Linscott). Anchor, NY, 1959 (pb)

DiPrima, Diane. "Various Fables from Various Places." Capricorn, NY, 1960 (pb)

――――. "This Kind of Bird Flies Backwards." Corinth, NY, 1967 (pb)

――――. "Dinners and Nightmares." Corinth, NY, 1961 (pb)

――――. "The New Handbook of Heaven." Auerhahn Press, SF, 1963 (pb)

――――. "Revolutionary Letters." Artists Workshop Press, Detroit, 1968 (pb)

———. "Memoirs of a Beatnik." Olympia Press, NY, 1969 (pb)

Donne, John. "Complete Poems" (ed. Fausset). Everyman, NY, 1936.

———. "Complete Poetry and Selected Prose." Modern Library, NY, 1946

———. "Selected Poetry" (ed. Bewley). Signet, NY, 1966 (pb)

Doxiadis, Constantin. "Urban Renewal and the Future of the American City." Public Administration Service, Chicago 1966 (pb)

———. "Architecture in Transition." OUP, NY, 1963 (pb)

———. "Ekistics." OUP, NY, 1968

———. "Between Dystopia and Utopia." Trinity, NY, 1966

Dreiser, Theodore. "An American Tragedy." Signet, NY, 1949 (pb)

———. "The Financier." Signet, NY, 1967 (pb)

———. "The Genius." Signet, NY, 1967 (pb)

———. "Jennie Gerhardt." Dell, NY, 1963 (pb)

———. "Sister Carrie." Signet, NY, 1962 (pb)

———. "Titan." Signet, NY, 1965 (pb)

———. "Letters of" (ed. Elias). U. of Pennsylvania, Philadelphia, 1959

Eberhardt, Richard. "Collected Poems, 1930–60." OUP, NY, 1969

———. "Collected Verse Plays." U. of N. Carolina Press, Chapel Hill, 1962

———. "Selected Poems: 1930–65." New Directions, NY, 1966 (pb)

Eigner, Larry. "On My Eyes." Jargon, Highlands, 1960

———. "From the Sustaining Air." Toad Press, Eugene, 1967 (pb)

———. "Another Time in Fragments." Fulcrum/Grossman, London/NY, 1967

Eisenstein, Sergei. "Film Form and The Film Sense." Meridian, NY, 1957 (pb)

———. "Ivan the Terrible." Simon & Schuster, NY, 1962

———. "Qué Viva Mexico!" Vision Press, London, 1951

Eliot, T. S. "Collected Poems, 1909–62." Harcourt, Brace, NY, 1963

———. "Complete Poems and Plays, 1909–50." Harcourt, Brace, NY, 1952

———. "Selected Essays." Harcourt, Brace, NY, 1950

———. "Selected Poems." Harbrace, NY, 1964 (pb)

———. "On Poetry and Cats." Noonday, NY, 1957 (pb)

———. "Waste Land and Other Poems." Harvest, NY, 1955 (pb)

Emerson, Ralph Waldo. "Complete Essays and Other Writings." Modern Library, NY, 1950

———. "Portable Emerson" (ed. van Doren). Viking, NY, 1946 (pb)

———. "Selected Writings" (ed. Gilman). Signet, NY, 1965 (pb)

Fromm, Erich. "The Art of Loving." Colophon, NY, 1956 (pb)

———. "Escape from Freedom." Avon, NY, 1969 (pb)

———. "Man for Himself." Premier, NY, 1968 (pb)

———. "Sane Society." Premier, NY, 1968 (pb)

———. "You Shall Be as Gods." Premier, NY, 1969 (pb)

Han-Shan. Translations of Han-Shan available in the following collections:

Waley, Arthur, ed./trs. "Chinese Poems." Unwin, London, 1961 (pb)

Snyder, Gary. "Riprap and Cold Mountain Poems." 4 Seasons, SF, 1965 (pb)

Hawthorne, Nathaniel. "The Celestial Railroad and Other Stories." Signet, NY, 1963 (pb)

———. "The Complete Short Stories." Doubleday, NY, 1959

———. "House of Seven Gables." Collier, NY, 1962 (pb)

———. "Novels and Tales." Modern Library, NY.

———. "The Scarlet Letter." Modern Library, NY, 1950

Hemingway, Ernest. "Collected poems." Haskell, NY, 1960 (pb)

———. "The Sun Also Rises." Scribner, NY, 1926 (pb)

———. "Farewell to Arms." Scribner, NY, 1929 (pb)

———. "In Our Time." Scribner, NY, 1930 (pb)

———. "The Fifth Column and Other Stories." Scribner NY, 1969

———. "Death in the Afternoon." Scribner, NY, 1969 (pb)

——. "For Whom the Bell Tolls. Scribner, NY, 1960 (pb)

——. "The Green Hills of Africa." Scribner, NY, 1935 (pb)

——. "A Movable Feast." NY, Scribner, NY, 1964

——. "The Old Man and the Sea." Scribner, NY, 1960

——. "The Short Stories." Scribner, NY, 1938 (pb)

——. "To Have and Have Not." Scribner, NY, 1937 (pb)

Hirschman, Jack. "YOD." Trigram, London, 1968

——. "NHR." Christopher Books, Santa Barbara, 1970

——. "Black Alephs." Trigram, London, 1969

——, tr. & ed. "Artaud Anthology." City Lights, SF, 1965

——. tr. w/Victor Erlich. "Electric Iron" (poems by Mayakovsky). Maya, SF, 1970

Homer. "Anger of Achilles" (tr. Graves). Doubleday, NY, 1959

——. "Complete Works." (ed. Miller & Shefter). Modern Library, NY.

——. "The Iliad." (tr. Rouse). Mentor, NY, 1956 (pb)

——. "The Odyssey" (tr. Rouse). New American Library, NY, 1963 (pb)

Hughes, Langston. "The Langston Hughes Reader." Braziller, NY, 1958

——. "Best of Simple." Hill & Wang, NY, 1961 (pb)

——. "The Big Sea." Hill & Wang, NY, 1963 (pb)

——. "Selected Poems." Knopf, NY, 1959

——. "Panther and the Lash." Vintage, NY, 1967 (pb)

——, ed. w/Arna Bontemps. "Poetry of the Negro, 1746–1949." Doubleday, NY, 1949

Huxley, Aldous. "Brave New World and Brave New World Revisited." Colophon, NY, 1958 (pb)

——. "Collected Essays." Bantam, NY, 1961 (pb)

——. "Collected Short Stories." Bantam, NY. (pb)

——. "Doors of Perception and Heaven and Hell." Colophon, NY, 1954 (pb)

——. "Island." Bantam, NY, 1963 (pb)

——. "Perennial Philosophy." Meridian, NY, 1962 (pb)

——. "Point Counter Point." Harper, NY, 1965 (pb)

――――. "Tomorrow and Tomorrow and Tomorrow." Signet, NY (pb)

――――. "The World of Aldous Huxley" (ed. Rollo). Universal, NY, 1966 (pb)

Isherwood, Christopher. "Berlin Stories." New Directions, NY, 1954 (pb)

――――. "Exhumations." Simon & Schuster, NY, 1966

――――. "Prater Violet." Ballantine Books, NY. (pb)

――――. "Ramakrishna and His Disciples." Simon & Schuster, NY, 1965

――――, ed. "Vedanta for the Western World." Compass, NY, 1969 (pb)

――――, ed. Vedanta for the Modern Man." Collier, NY, 1962 (pb)

Jeffers, Robinson. "The Beginning and the End." Random House, NY, 1963

――――. "Selected Poetry." Random House, NY, 1938

――――. "Selected Poems." Vintage, NY, 1965 (pb)

――――. "Selected Letters, 1897–1962." Johns Hopkins Press, Baltimore, 1968

――――. "Not Man Apart" (ed. Brower). Ballantine Books, NY, 1969 (pb)

Jolas, Eugene. "The Language of Night." Servire Press, The Hague, 1932

――――, ed. "Transition Workshop." Vanguard, NY, 1949

――――, ed. "Vertical: Yearbook of Romantic Mystic Ascensions." Gotham, Book Mart, NY, 1941

Jones, LeRoi. "Black Magic Poetry." Bobbs-Merrill, NY, 1969

――――. "Black Music." Apollo, NY, 1968 (pb)

――――. "Blues People." Apollo, NY, 1963 (pb)

――――. "The Dead Lecturer." Evergreen, NY, 1964 (pb)

――――. "Four Black Revolutionary Plays." Bobbs-Merrill, NY, 1969 (pb)

――――. "Home: Social Essays." Apollo, NY, 1967 (pb)

――――. "System of Dante's Hell." Grove, NY, 1965 (pb)

――――. "Preface to a 20 Volume Suicide Note." Corinth/Citadel, NY, 1961 (pb)

――――. "Tales." Grove, NY, 1968 (pb)

Joyce, James. "Ulysses." Vintage, NY, 1968 (pb)

———. "Finnegans Wake." Compass, NY, 1961 (pb)

———. "Collected Poems." Compass, NY, 1957 (pb)

———. "Critical Writings" (ed. Mason & Ellmann). Viking, NY, 1959 (pb)

———. "Dubliners." Compass, NY, 1958 (pb)

———. "Exiles." Compass, NY, 1961 (pb)

———. "Portrait of the Artist as a Young Man." Compass, NY, 1964 (pb)

———. "Letters" (3 vols., ed. Gilbert & Ellman). Viking Press, NY, 1957–66

Kelly, Robert, "Finding the Measure." Black Sparrow Press, LA, 1969 (pb)

———. "The Common Shore." Black Sparrow Press, LA, 1969

———, ed. w/Paris Leary. "A Controversy of Poets." Anchor, NY, 1965 (pb)

———. "Axon Dendron Tree." Matter, Annandale-on-Hudson, NY, 1967

Kunitz, Stanley. "Selected Poems, 1928–58." Little, Brown, NY, 1958 (pb)

Lawrence, D. H. "Apocalypse." Compass, NY, 1966 (pb)

———. "Collected Letters" (2 vols., ed. Moore). Viking, NY, 1962

———. "Complete Plays." Viking, NY, 1966

———. "Complete Poems" (2 vols., ed. Roberts & Pinto). Viking, NY, 1964

———. "Complete Short Stories." (3 vols.). Compass, NY, 1961 (pb)

———. "Lady Chatterley's Lover." Grove, NY, 1962 (pb)

———. "Plumed Serpent." Vintage, NY, 1951 (pb)

———. "Phoenix: I & II: The Posthumous Papers" (2 vols., ed. Roberts, Moore, & MacDonald). Viking, NY, 1966–67

———. "Portable D. H. Lawrence" (ed. Trilling). Compass, NY, 1947 (pb)

———. "Sons and Lovers." Compass, NY, 1958 (pb)

———. "Studies in Classic American Literature." Compass, NY, 1964 (pb)

Lindsay, Vachel. "Adventures, Rhymes and Designs." Eakins, NY, 1968

―――. "Collected Poems." Macmillan, NY, 1925

―――. "Selected Poems" (ed. Harris). Collier, NY, 1963 (pb)

―――. "Johnny Appleseed and Other Poems." Macmillan, NY, 1928

Lowell, Robert. "For the Union Dead." Noonday, NY, 1964 (pb)

―――. "Imitations." Noonday, NY, 1961 (pb)

―――. "Life Studies." Noonday, NY, 1967 (pb)

―――. "Mills of the Kavanaugh and Lord Weary's Castle." Harvest, NY, 1968 pb)

―――. "Old Glory." Noonday, NY, 1965 (pb)

Lowenfels, Walter. "Some Deaths." Jargon, Highlands, 1964 (pb)

―――. "To an Imaginary Daughter." Horizon, NY, 1964

―――. "Portable" (ed. Gover). International Publishers, 1968 (pb)

―――, ed. "Poets of Today." International Publishers, NY, 1964 (pb)

―――, ed. "Where Is Vietnam?" Doubleday, NY, 1967 (pb)

Mailer, Norman. "Advertisements for Myself." Signet, NY, 1959 (pb)

―――. "American Dream." Dell, NY, 1966 (pb)

―――. "Barbary Shore." University, NY, 1963 (pb); Signet, NY, 1960 (pb)

―――. "Cannibals and Christians." Dell, NY, 1967 (pb)

―――. "Deer Park." Dell, NY, 1967 (pb)

―――. "Naked and The Dead." Modern Library, NY, 1948; NAL, NY, 1954 (pb)

―――. "Short Fiction of." Dell, NY, 1967 (pb)

―――. "Why Are We in Vietnam?" Dell, NY, 1968 (pb)

―――. "Miami and the Siege of Chicago." Signet, NY, 1968 (pb)

Melville, Herman. "Confidence Man." Signet, NY, 1954 (pb)

―――. "Mardi." Signet, NY, 1964 (pb)

―――. "Moby Dick." Washington Square, NY, 1961, (pb)

―――. "Pierre, or The Ambiguities." Grove Press, NY, 1957 (pb)

——. "Portable Melville" (ed. Leyda). Compass, NY, 1952 (pb)

——. "Selected Writings." Modern Library, NY.

——. "Selected Poems of" (ed. Cohen). S. Illinois U., Carbondale, 1964 (pb)

——. "Works of" (16 vols.). Russell & Russell, NY, 1922–24; reprint, 1963

Merton, Thomas. "Bread in the Wilderness" (rev. ed.). New Directions, NY, 1960 (pb)

——. "Cables to the Ace." New Directions, NY, 1968 (pb)

——. "Conjectures of a Guilty Bystander." Doubleday, NY, 1966 (pb)

——. "Disputed Questions." Farrar, Straus & Giroux, NY, 1960 (pb)

——. "Disputed Questions." Farrar, Straus & Giroux, NY, 1960 (pb)

——. "Emblems of a Season of Fury." New Directions, NY, 1963 (pb)

——. "Mystics and Zen Masters." Delta, NY, 1969 (pb)

——. "Raids on the Unspeakable." New Directions, NY, 1970 (pb)

——. "Selected Poems." New Directions, NY, 1967 (pb)

——. "Seven Storey Mountain." Signet, NY, 1961 (pb)

Milarepa. "Message of" (ed. Clarke). Paragon, NY.

——. "The One Hundred Thousand Songs" (2 vols., tr. Chang). University Books, NY, 1962

Miller, Henry. "Big Sur and The Oranges of Hieronymus Bosch." New Direction, NY, 1964 (pb)

——. "The Books in My Life." New Directions, NY, 1969 (pb)

——. "Black Spring." Grove Press, NY, 1963 (pb)

——. "Colossus of Maroussi." New Directions, NY, 1958 (pb)

——. "Cosmological Eye." New Directions, NY, 1961 (pb)

——. "Nexus, Plexus, Sexus: The Rosy Crucifixion" (3 vols.). Grove Press, NY, 1965 (pb)

——. "Tropic of Cancer." Grove Press, NY, 1961 (pb)

——. "Tropic of Capricorn." Grove Press, NY, 1962 (pb)

———. "Time of the Assassins." New Directions, NY, 1962 (pb)

Milton, John. "Portable Milton" (ed. Bush). Viking, NY, 1949 (pb)

———. "Complete English Poetry of" (ed. Shawcross). Anchor, NY, 1961

———. "Paradise Lost and Other Poems." Mentor, NY, 1963 (pb)

Moody, William Vaughn. "Poems and Plays." AMS, NY, 1969

———. "Some Letters." AMS, NY, 1969

———. "Selected Poems." Houghton Mifflin, Boston, 1931

Morris, William. "News from Nowhere." Monthly Review Press, NY, 1966

———. "Selected Writings and Designs" (ed. Briggs). Penguin, Baltimore, 1962 (pb)

———. "Selected Writings" (ed. Cole). Random House, NY.

———. "Three Works by." International Publishers, NY, 1968 (pb)

———. "Wood Beyond the World." Ballantine Books, NY, 1969

Neruda, Pablo. "Bestiary" (tr. Neuberger). Harcourt, Brace, NY, 1965

———. "Heights of Machu Picchu" (tr. Tarn). Noonday, NY, 1967 (pb)

———. "Selected Poems" (tr. Bellit). Grove, NY, 1961 (pb)

———. "A New Decade" (tr. Bellit & Reid). Grove, NY, 1969

———. "We Are Many" (tr. Reid). Grossman, NY, 1968 (pb)

———. "20 Poems" (tr. Bly & Wright). Sixties Press, Madison, 1967 (pb)

———. "20 Love Poems and a Song of Despair" (tr. Merwin). Grossman, NY, 1969 (pb)

Nin, Anaïs. "Dairy of, 1931–34." Harcourt, Brace, NY, 1968 (pb)

———. "Diary of, 1935–39." Harcourt, Brace, NY, 1969, (pb)

———. "D. H. Lawrence: An Unprofessional Study." Swallow, Denver, 1964 (pb)

———. "Novel of the Future." Macmillan, NY, 1968

———. "Spy in the House of Love." Swallow, Denver, 1959 (pb)

Nordhoff, Charles Hall, & James Norman. "Bounty Trilogy." Little, Brown, NY, 1946

———. "Falcons of France." Little, Brown, NY, 1929

———. "Men Against the Sea." Pocket Books, NY, 1968 (pb)

———. "Mutiny on the Bounty." Pocket Books, NY, 1956 (pb)

———. "Pitcairn's Island." Pocket Books, NY, 1958 (pb)

Olson, Charles. "A Bibliography on America for Ed Dorn." 4 Seasons, SF, 1964 (pb)

———. "Call Me Ishmael." City Lights, SF, 1968 (pb)

———. "Casual Mythology." City Lights, SF, 1969 (pb)

———. "Distances." Grove, NY, 1960 (pb)

———. "Human Universe and Other Essays." Grove, NY, 1968 (pb)

———. "In Cold Hell, in Thicket." 4 Seasons, SF, 1969 (pb)

———. "Letter for Origin" (ed. Glover). Grossman, NY, 1970 (pb)

———. "Maximus Poems." Corinth, NY, 1960 (pb)

———. "Maximus, 4, 5 & 6." Grossman, NY, 1969 (pb)

———. "Mayan Letters." Grossman, NY, 1968 (pb)

———. "Proprioception." 4 Seasons, SF, 1965 (pb)

———. "Reading at Berkeley." Coyote, SF, 1966 (pb)

———. "Selected Writings" (ed. Creeley). New Directions, NY, 1967 (pb)

Oppenheim, James. "Nine-Tenths." Gregg Reprints, NY, 1969

Patchen, Kenneth. "Because It Is." New Directions, NY, 1960 (pb)

———. "But Even So." New Directions, NY, 1968 (pb)

———. "The Collected Poems." New Directions, NY, 1969 (pb)

———. "Doubleheader." New Directions, NY, 1966 (pb)

———. "Hallelujah Anyway." New Directions, NY, 1966 (pb)

———. "Journal of Albion Moonlight." New Directions, NY, 1961 (pb)

———. "Love Poems." City Lights, SF, 1960 (pb)

———. "Memoirs of a Shy Pornographer." New Directions, NY, 1965 (pb)

———. "Sleepers Awake." New Directions, NY, 1969 (pb)

Po Chu-i. Translations of Po Chu-i available in the following collections:

Waley, Arthur, ed./tr. "Chinese Poems." Unwin, London, 1961 (pb)

———. "170 Chinese Poems." Knopf, NY, 1923

———. "Life and Times of Po Chu-i." Hillary, NY, 1949

Payne, Robert, ed. "The White Pony: An Anthology of Chinese Poetry." Mentor, NY, 1960 (pb)

Bynner, Witter, ed. "The Jade Mountain." Anchor, NY, 1964 (pb)

Pound, Ezra. "The ABC of Reading." New Directions, NY, 1960 (pb)

———. "Cantos: 1–95." New Directions, NY, 1965

———. "Guide to Kulchur." New Directions, NY, 1968 (pb)

———. "Letters of, 1907–41" (ed. Page). Harvest, NY, 1962? (pb)

———. "Literary Essays" (ed. Eliot). New Directions, NY, 1968, (pb)

———. "Personae: Collected Shorter Poems." New Directions, NY, 1950

———. "The Spirit of Romance." New Directions, NY, 1968 (pb)

———. "Translations." New Directions, NY, 1953, (pb)

———. "Confucian Odes." New Directions, NY, 1959 (pb)

———. "Confucius: The Unwobbling Pivot and the Great Digest." New Directions, NY, 1969 (pb)

———, ed. Fenollosa. "The Chinese Written Character as a Medium for Poetry." City Lights, SF, 1936 (pb)

Powell, Lawrence Clark. "Fortune and Friendship." Bowker, NY, 1968

———. "Robinson Jeffers." Haskell Reprints, NY, 1969

Ransom, John Crowe. "Poems and Essays." Vintage, NY, 196— (pb)

————. "Selected Poems." Knopf, NY, 1969

————. "World's Body." Louisiana State, Baton Rouge, 1968 (pb)

————, ed. "Kenyon Critics." Kennikat, NY, 1951

Reich, Wilhelm. "Character Analysis." Noonday, NY, 1949 (pb)

————. "Function of the Orgasm." Noonday, NY, 1961 (pb)

————. "Listen, Little Man!" Noonday, NY, 1969 (pb)

————. "Murder of Christ." Noonday, NY, 1970 (pb)

————. "Reich Speaks of Freud." Noonday, NY, 1967 (pb)

————. "Selected Writings." Noonday, NY, 1960 (pb)

————. "The Sexual Revolution." Noonday, NY, 1963 (pb)

Riesman, David. "Abundance for What?" Anchor, NY, 1965 (pb)

————. "Faces in the Crowd." Yale, New Haven, 1952 (pb)

————. "Individualism Reconsidered." Free Press, NY, 1954 (pb)

————. "The Lonely Crowd." Yale, New Haven, 1950 (pb)

Roethke,, Theodore. "Collected Poems." Doubleday, Garden City, NY, 1966

————. "Far Field." Doubleday, NY, 1964

————. "On the Poet and His Craft" (ed. Mills). U. of Washington, Seattle, 1965 (pb)

————. "Selected Letters" (ed. Mills). U. of Washington, Seattle, 1968

————. "Words for the Wind." Indiana U. Press, Bloomington, 1961 (pb)

Sandburg, Carl. "Always the Young Strangers." Harcourt, Brace, NY, 1953

————. "Complete Poems." Harcourt, Brace, NY, 1970

————. "Harvest Poems." Harvest, NY, 1960 (pb)

————. "The People, Yes." Harcourt, Brace, NY, 1936

————. "Poems of the Midwest." World, NY, 1946 (pb)

————. "Letters of" (ed. Mitgang). Harcourt, Brace, NY, 1968

Service, Robert W. "Collected Poems." Dodd, Mead, NY, 1944

———. "Best of." Apollo, NY, 1953 (pb)

———. "Later Collected Verse." Dodd, Mead, NY, 1965

———. "More Collected Verse." Dodd, Mead, NY, 1965

Seton, Ernest Thompson. "Animal Heroes." Grosset, NY, 1951 (pb)

———. "Animal Tracks and Hunter Signs." Doubleday, NY, 1958

———. "Biography of a Grizzly." Schocken, NY, 1967 (pb)

———. "Ernest Thompson Seton's America." (ed. Wiley). Devin-Adair, NY, Seton, 1954, (pb)

———. "Lives of Game Animals." (8 vols.). Branford, Boston, Mass., 1953

———. "Two Little Savages." Dover, NY, 1963 (pb)

———. "Wild Animals I Have Known." Schocken, NY, 1966 (pb)

———. "Lives of the Hunted." Schocken, NY, 1967 (pb)

Spender, Stephen. "Collected Poems." Random House, NY, 1955

———. "Making of a Poem." Norton, NY, 1962 (pb)

———. "Selected Poetry." Random House, NY, 1964 (pb)

———. "World Within World." U. of Calif. Press, Berkeley, 1951 (pb)

———. "Year of Young Rebels." Vintage, NY, 1969 (pb)

Stein, Gertrude. "Autobiography of Alice B. Toklas." Vintage, NY, 1960 (pb)

———. "Collected Writings." Modern Library, NY.

———. "Geography and Plays." Something Else, NY, 1968, (pb)

———. "Three Lives." Vintage, NY, 0000 (pb)

———. "Lectures in America." Beacon, Boston, 1957 (pb)

———. "What Are Masterpieces?" Pitman, NY, 1969 (pb)

———. "The Making of Americans." Something Else, NY, 1966

———. "The Making of Americans" (abridged). Harvest, NY, 1966 (pb)

Sterling, George. "Selected Poems." Reprint House International, NY, 1923

———. "Sonnets to Craig." AMS, NY, 1928

———. "Truth." AMS, NY, 1931

Stock, Robert. "Covenants." Trident, NY, 1967

Tate, Allen. "Fathers." Swallow, Denver, 1960 (pb)

———. "Poems." Swallow, Denver, 1961 (pb)

———. "Stonewall Jackson." Ann Arbor, Ann Arbor, 1957 (pb)

Twain, Mark. "Adventures of Huckleberry Finn." Signet, NY, 1959 (pb)

———. "Adventures of Tom Sawyer." Dell, NY, 1967 (pb)

———. "Complete Essays" (ed. Neider). Doubleday, NY, 1963

———. "Complete Humorous Sketches and Tales" (ed. Neider). Doubleday, NY, 1961

———. "Short Stories of" (ed. Neider). Doubleday, NY, 1957

———. "Travel Books of" (2 vols., ed. Neider). Doubleday, NY.

———. "Life on the Mississippi." Signet, NY, 1961 (pb)

———. "The Mysterious Stranger." Signet, NY, 1962 (pb)

Vallejo, César. "Poemas Humanos" (tr. Eshleman). Grove, NY, 1968 (pb)

Warren, Robert Penn. "All the King's Men." Bantam, NY, 1959 (pb)

———. "Selected Poems, 1923–66." Random House, NY, 1966

———. "Selected Essays, 1934–43." OUP, NY, 1962

Weil, Simone. "Gravity and Grace." Humanities, NY, 1952 (pb)

———. "Selected Essays, 1934–43." OUP, NY, 1962

———. "70 Letters" (tr. Rees). OUP, NY, 1965

Whitman, Walt. "Leaves of Grass" (ed. Cowley). Compass, NY, 1961 (pb)

———. "Whitman Reader" (ed. Geismar). Pocket Books, NY, 1955 (pb)

———. "Complete Poetry and Selected Prose of" (ed. Miller). Houghton, Mifflin, Boston, 1960 (pb)

Williams, William Carlos. "Autobiography." New Directions, NY, 1967? (pb)

———. "Collected Earlier Poems." New Directions, NY, 1951

———. "Collected Later Poems." New Directions, NY, 1963

———. "Farmer's Daughter: Collected Short Stories." New Directions, NY, 1961 (pb)

———. "In the American Grain." New Directions, NY, 1956 (pb)

———. "Paterson: Books 1–5." New Directions, NY, 1951 (pb)

———. "Pictures from Breughel." New Directions, NY, 1967 (pb)

———. "Selected Essays." New Directions, NY, 1969 (pb)

———. "Spring and All." Frontier, Buffalo, 1970 (pb)

———. "Kora in Hell." City Lights, SF, 1957 (pb)

Wittgenstein, Ludwig. "Blue and Brown Books." Torchbooks, NY, 1965 (pb)

———. "Notebooks: 1914–16." Torchbooks, NY, 1969 (pb)

———. "On Certainty." Harper & Row, NY, 1970

———. "Tractatus Logico-Philosophicus." Humanities, NY, 1961

Yeats, William Butler. "Autobiography." Macmillan, NY, 1953 (pb)

———. "Celtic Twilight." Signet, NY, 1962 (pb)

———. "Collected Plays." (rev. ed.). Macmillan, NY, 1953

———. "Collected Poems." (definitive ed.). Macmillan, NY, 1951

———. "Eleven Plays." Collier, NY, 1968 (pb)

———. "Selected Poems." Macmillan, NY, 1962 (pb)

———. "A Vision." Macmillan, NY, 1956 (pb)

———. "Essays and Introductions." Macmillan, NY, 1961

———. "Irish Folk Stories and Fairy Tales." Universal, NY, 1957 (pb)

———. "Mythologies." Macmillan, NY, 1969

Zukofsky, Louis. "A: 1–12." Doubleday, NY, 1967

———. "A: 13–21." Doubleday, NY, 1969

———. "All: The Collected Shorter Poems, 1923–58." Norton, NY, 1965 (pb)

————. "All: The Collected Shorter Poems, 1956–64." Norton, NY, 1966 (pb)

————. "Prepositions." Horizon, NY, 1967

————. "Bottom: On Shakespeare" (2 vols., w/ Celia Zukofsky). Ark Press, Austin, 1963

————. "A Test of Poetry." Corinth, NY, 1964 (pb)

————. "Ferdinand." Grossman, NY, 1969 (pb)